D1450256

◆ ANCIENT WORLD LEADERS ◆

ALEXANDER THE GREAT

ATTILA THE HUN

JULIUS CAESAR

CHARLEMAGNE

GENGHIS KHAN

SALADIN

CHARLEMAGNE

Dale Evva Gelfand

CHELSEA HOUSE
PUBLISHERS
A Haights Cross Communications Company

Philadelphia

Frontispiece: A portrait of Charlemagne, the Holy Roman Emperor and "Father of Europe."

CHELSEA HOUSE PUBLISHERS

VP, NEW PRODUCT DEVELOPMENT Sally Cheney
DIRECTOR OF PRODUCTION Kim Shinners
CREATIVE MANAGER Takeshi Takahashi
MANUFACTURING MANAGER Diann Grasse

Staff for CHARLEMAGNE

ASSOCIATE EDITOR Benjamin Xavier Kim
PRODUCTION EDITOR Jaimie Winkler
PHOTO EDITOR Sarah Bloom
SERIES AND COVER DESIGNER Takeshi Takahashi
LAYOUT 21st Century Publishing and Communications, Inc.

A Haights Cross Communications Company

http://www.chelseahouse.com

First Printing

1 3 5 7 9 8 6 4 2

Library of Congress Cataloging-in-Publication Data

Gelfand, Dale Evva, 1944–
    Charlemagne / by Dale Evva Gelfand.
        p. cm.—(Ancient world leaders)
Includes index.
    ISBN 0-7910-7224-X
    1. Charlemagne, Emperor, 742–814—Juvenile literature. 2. Holy Roman Empire—Kings and rulers—Biography—Juvenile literature. 3. France—History—To 987—Juvenile literature. 4. Civilization, Medieval—Juvenile literature. I. Title. II. Series.
DC73 .G38 2002
944'.014'092—dc21

2002015905

TABLE OF CONTENTS

ON LEADERSHIP

Arthur M. Schlesinger, jr.

Leadership, it may be said, is really what makes the world go round. Love no doubt smoothes the passage; but love is a private transaction between consenting adults. Leadership is a public transaction with history. The idea of leadership affirms the capacity of individuals to move, inspire, and mobilize masses of people so that they act together in pursuit of an end. Sometimes leadership serves good purposes, sometimes bad; but whether the end is benign or evil, great leaders are those men and women who leave their personal stamp on history.

Now, the very concept of leadership implies the proposition that individuals can make a difference. This proposition has never been universally accepted. From classical times to the present day, eminent thinkers have regarded individuals as no more than the agents and pawns of larger forces, whether the gods and goddesses of the ancient world or, in the modern era, race, class, nation, the dialectic, the will of the people, the spirit of the times, history itself. Against such forces, the individual dwindles into insignificance.

So contends the thesis of historical determinism. Tolstoy's great novel *War and Peace* offers a famous statement of the case. Why, Tolstoy asked, did millions of men in the Napoleonic Wars, denying their human feelings and their common sense, move back and forth across Europe slaughtering their fellows? "The war," Tolstoy answered, "was bound to happen simply because it was bound to happen." All prior history determined it. As for leaders, they, Tolstoy said, "are but the labels that serve to give a name to an end and, like labels, they have the least possible connection with the event." The greater the leader, "the more conspicuous the inevitability and the predestination of every act he commits." The leader, said Tolstoy, is "the slave of history."

Determinism takes many forms. Marxism is the determinism of class. Nazism the determinism of race. But the idea of men and women as the slaves of history runs athwart the deepest human instincts. Rigid determinism abolishes the idea of human freedom—the assumption of free choice that underlies every move we make, every word we speak, every thought we think. It abolishes the idea of human responsibility, since it is manifestly unfair to reward or punish people for actions that are by definition beyond their control. No one can live consistently by any deterministic creed. The Marxist states prove this themselves by their extreme susceptibility to the cult of leadership.

More than that, history refutes the idea that individuals make no difference. In December 1931 a British politician crossing Fifth Avenue in New York City between 76th and 77th Streets around 10:30 P.M. looked in the wrong direction and was knocked down by an automobile—a moment, he later recalled, of a man aghast, a world aglare: "I do not understand why I was not broken like an eggshell or squashed like a gooseberry." Fourteen months later an American politician, sitting in an open car in Miami, Florida, was fired on by an assassin; the man beside him was hit. Those who believe that individuals make no difference to history might well ponder whether the next two decades would have been the same had Mario Constasino's car killed Winston Churchill in 1931 and Giuseppe Zangara's bullet killed Franklin Roosevelt in 1933. Suppose, in addition, that Lenin had died of typhus in Siberia in 1895 and that Hitler had been killed on the western front in 1916. What would the 20th century have looked like now?

For better or for worse, individuals do make a difference. "The notion that a people can run itself and its affairs anonymously," wrote the philosopher William James, "is now well known to be the silliest of absurdities. Mankind does nothing save through initiatives on the part of inventors, great or small, and imitation by the rest of us—these are the sole factors in human progress. Individuals of genius show the way, and set the patterns, which common people then adopt and follow."

Leadership, James suggests, means leadership in thought as well as in action. In the long run, leaders in thought may well make the greater difference to the world. "The ideas of economists and political philosophers, both when they are right and when they are wrong," wrote John Maynard Keynes, "are more powerful than is commonly understood. Indeed the world is ruled by little else. Practical men, who believe themselves to be quite exempt from any intellectual influences, are usually the slaves of some defunct economist. . . . The power of vested interests is vastly exaggerated compared with the gradual encroachment of ideas."

But, as Woodrow Wilson once said, "Those only are leaders of men, in the general eye, who lead in action. . . . It is at their hands that new thought gets its translation into the crude language of deeds." Leaders in thought often invent in solitude and obscurity, leaving to later generations the tasks of imitation. Leaders in action—the leaders portrayed in this series—have to be effective in their own time.

And they cannot be effective by themselves. They must act in response to the rhythms of their age. Their genius must be adapted, in a phrase from William James, "to the receptivities of the moment." Leaders are useless without followers. "There goes the mob," said the French politician, hearing a clamor in the streets. "I am their leader. I must follow them." Great leaders turn the inchoate emotions of the mob to purposes of their own. They seize on the opportunities of their time, the hopes, fears, frustrations, crises, potentialities. They succeed when events have prepared the way for them, when the community is awaiting to be aroused, when they can provide the clarifying and organizing ideas. Leadership completes the circuit between the individual and the mass and thereby alters history.

It may alter history for better or for worse. Leaders have been responsible for the most extravagant follies and most monstrous crimes that have beset suffering humanity. They have also been vital in such gains as humanity has made in individual freedom, religious and racial tolerance, social justice, and respect for human rights.

There is no sure way to tell in advance who is going to lead for good and who for evil. But a glance at the gallery of men and women in ANCIENT WORLD LEADERS suggests some useful tests.

One test is this: Do leaders lead by force or by persuasion? By command or by consent? Through most of history leadership was exercised by the divine right of authority. The duty of followers was to defer and to obey. "Theirs not to reason why/Theirs but to do and die." On occasion, as with the so-called enlightened despots of the 18th century in Europe, absolutist leadership was animated by humane purposes. More often, absolutism nourished the passion for domination, land, gold, and conquest and resulted in tyranny.

The great revolution of modern times has been the revolution of equality. "Perhaps no form of government," wrote the British historian James Bryce in his study of the United States, *The American Commonwealth,* "needs great leaders so much as democracy." The idea that all people should be equal in their legal condition has undermined the old structure of authority, hierarchy, and deference. The revolution of equality has had two contrary effects on the nature of leadership. For equality, as Alexis de Tocqueville pointed out in his great study *Democracy in America*, might mean equality in servitude as well as equality in freedom.

"I know of only two methods of establishing equality in the political world," Tocqueville wrote. "Rights must be given to every citizen, or none at all to anyone . . . save one, who is the master of all." There was no middle ground "between the sovereignty of all and the absolute power of one man." In his astonishing prediction of 20th-century totalitarian dictatorship, Tocqueville explained how the revolution of equality could lead to the *Führerprinzip* and more terrible absolutism than the world had ever known.

But when rights are given to every citizen and the sovereignty of all is established, the problem of leadership takes a new form, becomes more exacting than ever before. It is easy to issue commands and enforce them by the rope and the stake, the concentration camp and the *gulag*. It is much harder to use argument and achievement to overcome opposition and win consent. The Founding Fathers of the United States understood the difficulty. They believed that history had given them the opportunity to decide, as Alexander Hamilton wrote in the first Federalist Paper, whether men are indeed capable of basing government on "reflection and choice, or whether they are forever destined to depend . . . on accident and force."

Government by reflection and choice called for a new style of leadership and a new quality of followership. It required leaders to be responsive to popular concerns, and it required followers to be active and informed participants in the process. Democracy does not eliminate emotion from politics; sometimes it fosters demagoguery; but it is confident that, as the greatest of democratic leaders put it, you cannot fool all of the people all of the time. It measures leadership by results and retires those who overreach or falter or fail.

It is true that in the long run despots are measured by results too. But they can postpone the day of judgment, sometimes indefinitely, and in the meantime they can do infinite harm. It is also true that democracy is no guarantee of virtue and intelligence in government, for the voice of the people is not necessarily the voice of God. But democracy, by assuring the right of opposition, offers built-in resistance to the evils inherent in absolutism. As the theologian Reinhold Niebuhr summed it up, "Man's capacity for justice makes democracy possible, but man's inclination to justice makes democracy necessary."

A second test for leadership is the end for which power is sought. When leaders have as their goal the supremacy of a master race or the promotion of totalitarian revolution or the acquisition and exploitation of colonies or the protection of greed and privilege or the preservation of personal power, it is likely that their leadership will do little to advance the cause of humanity. When their goal is the abolition of slavery, the liberation of women, the enlargement of opportunity for the poor and powerless, the extension of equal rights to racial minorities, the defense of the freedoms of expression and opposition, it is likely that their leadership will increase the sum of human liberty and welfare.

Leaders have done great harm to the world. They have also conferred great benefits. You will find both sorts in this series. Even "good" leaders must be regarded with a certain wariness. Leaders are not demigods; they put on their trousers one leg after another just like ordinary mortals. No leader is infallible, and every leader needs to be reminded of this at regular intervals. Irreverence irritates leaders but is their salvation. Unquestioning submission corrupts leaders and demeans followers. Making a cult of a leader is always a mistake. Fortunately hero worship generates its own antidote. "Every hero," said Emerson, "becomes a bore at last."

The single benefit the great leaders confer is to embolden the rest of us to live according to our own best selves, to be active, insistent, and resolute in affirming our own sense of things. For great leaders attest to the reality of human freedom against the supposed inevitabilities of history. And they attest to the wisdom and power that may lie within the most unlikely of us, which is why Abraham Lincoln remains the supreme example of great leadership. A great leader, said Emerson, exhibits new possibilities to all humanity. "We feed on genius . . . . Great men exist that there may be greater men."

Great leaders, in short, justify themselves by emancipating and empowering their followers. So humanity struggles to master its destiny, remembering with Alexis de Tocqueville: "It is true that around every man a fatal circle is traced beyond which he cannot pass; but within the wide verge of that circle he is powerful and free; as it is with man, so with communities." ■

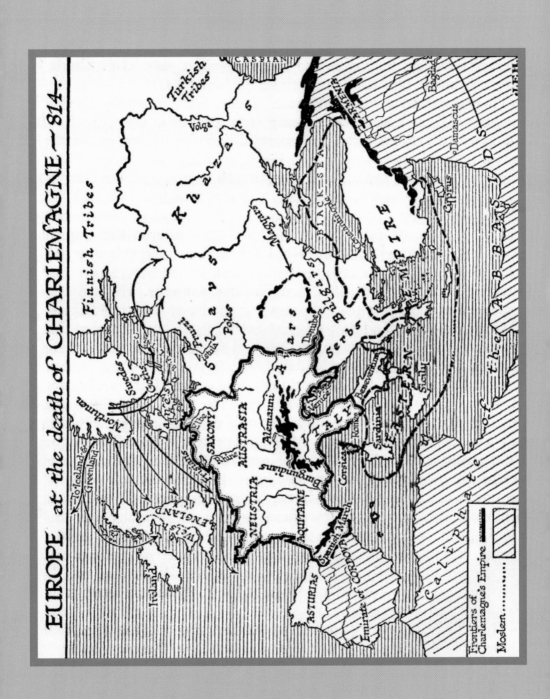

EUROPE at the death of CHARLEMAGNE ~ 814.

Turkish Tribes

Finnish Tribes

Volga

Khazars

Caucasus

CASPIAN

ARMENIA

Bagdad

Damascus

Cyprus

BLACK SEA

Constantinople

Magyars

Danube

Bulgars

Serbs

A v a r s

Dnieper

Don

I H L

D

S

B

A

B

B

A

e

h

t

f

o

e

t

a

h

P

i

l

a

C

EASTERN EMPIRE

Swedes & Goths

Northmen

Iceland & Greenland

Ireland

WELSH

ENGLAND

Frisians

Slavs

Poles

Vistula

Pruzzi

Danes

Elbe

SAXONY

AUSTRASIA

Rhine

Alemanni

NEUSTRIA

AQUITAINE

Burgundians

ITALY

Venice

Rome

Beneventum

Corsica

Sardinia

Sicily

ASTURIAS

Emirate of CORDOVA

Spanish March

Frontiers of
Charlemagne's Empire ——————
Moslem..........

1

HOLY ROMAN EMPEROR

On Christmas Day in the year 800, during a mass being celebrated in Saint Peter's Basilica in Rome by Pope Leo III, the foremost event in the very eventful life of Charlemagne, king of the Franks, took place. Perhaps in hindsight, the legendary conqueror and defender of Christendom might have expected that something out of the ordinary would happen. During the preceding month, Charlemagne had taken action on a crisis that threatened the unity of the Roman Church—the forced removal of the pope—and averted it. At the very least, Charlemagne (French for "Charles the Great") might have assumed that the mass would be a particularly notable one. Only days earlier Pope Leo had managed to hold onto his exalted office—so he would most certainly be in a celebratory mood. What Charlemagne didn't expect was that he himself would play a starring role in the day's pageantry.

Having entered the church merely to participate in Christmas

An illuminated manuscript depicting Charlemagne's coronation by Pope Leo III at St. Peter's Basilica in Rome. This event was not only monumental in Charlemagne's own personal history but that of all Western rulers, for Charlemagne was the first ruler to be dubbed Holy Roman Emperor since the fifth century.

mass, the 58-year-old Charlemagne approached the high altar—beneath which lay the body of Saint Peter—and knelt to pray. Suddenly the pope, without warning, stepped forward and placed the imperial gold crown on Charlemagne's head. He anointed him Emperor of the Romans, honoring him as Augustus. Charlemagne thus became the first Western ruler to assume the title since the fifth century.

Charlemagne's fellow worshipers—all high-ranking clerics and noble Romans—immediately raised their voices in a congratulatory chorus, acclaiming: *"Carolo Augusto, a Deo coronato, mango et pacifico imperatori, vita et vicotria"*

("Charles Augustus, crowned by God, the pacific emperor, life and victory.") This was repeated three times, whereupon Pope Leo placed the imperial cloak over Charlemagne's shoulders and then prostrated himself before the new emperor. It was the only time in the history of the papacy that a pope bowed before a mortal king. He then venerated Charlemagne in accordance with the imperial coronation rituals that had been established by the ancient emperors. Leo concluded the ceremony by anointing Charlemagne with holy oil. Thus on the sacred day of Christ's nativity, Charlemagne, undisputed ruler of western Europe and Christendom's staunchest defender and supporter, was crowned Roman Emperor.

(After Charlemagne's death the title would become known as Holy Roman Emperor—the last emperor to try to assume the title would be Napoleon I in 1804. Likewise, the territory would some four centuries later be designated the Holy Roman Empire, recognizing the enduring bond between church and state. But it was "holy" only as a way for the popes who came after Leo to justify their religious control in Europe. And it was called "Roman Empire" as a reminder of the original Roman Empire's political power in the West as a way to offset the might of the Byzantine Empire in the East. Neither term, in fact, was apt.)

The *Annales Laureshamenses,* a contemporary monastic account, asserts that God had seen fit to aid Charlemagne in conquering the realms of Saxony, Bavaria, Avars (modern Austria and Hungary), France, Lombardy, and Rome, putting them under his power. Therefore, it seemed equally fitting to Pope Leo and the priests and other good Christians who were present at the council that Charlemagne should hold the title of emperor. This was particularly true since a woman—the Empress Irene—now claimed the imperial authority. Not wanting to refuse "their petition and humbly submitting himself to God and to the petition of all the Christian priests and people," Charlemagne accepted and was consecrated Roman Emperor by Pope Leo III.

However, unlike the old Roman Empire, this new one had been created by and for the Church itself. This made the empire subordinate to the Church. Likewise, the newly crowned Roman Emperor was subordinate to the pope. The coronation completed the merger between the Frankish monarchy and the Church that was begun by Charlemagne's father, Pepin. Furthermore, according to historian Keith Tankard, "The coronation also meant that the political alliance of the Papacy was no longer divided between the lawful authority of the Byzantines and the de facto power of Charlemagne. The Church now enjoyed peace, authority, influence, and prestige, which it had not since the time of Gregory, because it was now subject to the zeal and vigilance of Charlemagne."

Even in his own day, Charlemagne was referred to as "the Great." Known also to his contemporaries as *Europae Pater,* or "Father of Europe," Charlemagne sowed the seeds of historical change. For the first time since the breakup of the Roman Empire in the West during the fourth and fifth centuries, a distinct European society emerged among the Franks in Gaul, largely abetted by Charlemagne's Carolingian dynasty.

Charlemagne was certainly physically imposing enough to lead the Roman Empire. He was a towering figure, literally as well as figuratively. In an era when the average man was about five feet tall, the new emperor stood six feet four. In *Einhard: The Life of Charlemagne,* Einhard, Charlemagne's biographer as well as his trusted confidante and adviser, described his king thusly: "[H]is height is well known to have been seven times the length of his foot." And he was powerfully built as well. Einhard describes the king as "large and strong and of lofty stature . . . the upper part of his head was round, his eyes very large and animated, nose a little long, hair fair, and face laughing and merry. Thus his appearance was always stately and dignified, whether he was standing or sitting."

Until the time of his coronation, Charlemagne dressed like his fellow Franks: linen shirt and linen breeches, over which he wore a wool tunic with silk fringe. In winter he wore a close-fitting coat of either otter or marten skins, and thrown over his shoulders was a blue cloak. Again, according to Einhard, "He despised foreign costumes, however handsome, and never allowed himself to be robed in them." However, on becoming emperor, Charlemagne conceded to dressing the part when receiving dignitaries by wearing embroidered *chlamys* (Grecian-style robes) fastened with gold buckles, "shoes bedecked with precious stones" and "his head crowned with a diadem of gold and gems."

Even prior to the tumultuous events that took place the month before his coronation, Charlemagne had in effect been preparing for his "promotion" for some time. In fact, his becoming emperor might almost be seen as a foregone conclusion, given his heritage, his victorious battles, and the history of the Roman Church during medieval times.

In the years leading up to the eighth century when Charlemagne's family rose to prominence, the Roman Church in Frankish Gaul had been weakening in importance and power. The Church's governing body often had to put up with interference by the Frankish kings who had succeeded Clovis I. Clovis (466–511), the king of the Franks who had united most of what is now France and western Germany, had himself converted to Christianity around 500. (As was common practice at the time, he then forced his subjects to also convert to his new faith.) Perhaps the greatest of the Merovingian kings (who are often referred to as the "Long-Haired Kings") Clovis passed on a significantly enlarged kingdom to his sons. They then proceeded to divide it between them. However, the later Merovingian kings were weak rulers who allowed the nobles to take control of the kingdom from them. The Carolingians, which was Charlemagne's family—he was known to his contemporaries as Carolus Magnus, and it's from this name that "Carolingian" was derived—was one of those noble families. It was headed up by Charlemagne's grandfather, Charles Martel. The Carolingians rose to a

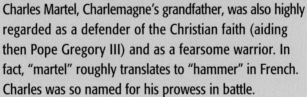

Charles Martel, Charlemagne's grandfather, was also highly regarded as a defender of the Christian faith (aiding then Pope Gregory III) and as a fearsome warrior. In fact, "martel" roughly translates to "hammer" in French. Charles was so named for his prowess in battle.

position of dominance while the Merovingians slipped in power and prestige.

At the same time, the Christian West had become isolated; Frankish Gaul was being threatened by Muslim invaders to the south and barbarians to the north. Banished to Spain in 721, the Muslims—or Saracens, as they were also known—had returned to France by 725, making inroads into the realm as far west as

Burgundy. There, yielding to the invaders' superior force, Duke Eudes III of Burgundy negotiated with the Saracens. He even gave his daughter in marriage to one of the Saracen chiefs.

Outraged by this surrender by the Burgundian duke, Charles Martel (or Charles the Hammer) took matters into his own hands. In October 732 in central France, he met in battle with Abd-er-Rahman, the governor of Spain. The governor had crossed the Pyrenees with an immense army that pillaged and burned towns as they advanced. According to the *Chronicle of Saint Denis,* the Muslims had planned to go to Tours to destroy first the Church of Saint Martin, then the city proper, and finally the entire Frankish kingdom in their mission to make Islam *the* one religion. However, Charles Martel defeated the invaders in what became known as the Battle of Tours (also known, more properly, as the Battle of Poitiers). It was a turning point in European history. Though it would have been unlikely for the Saracens, even if victorious, to have continued far into the northern kingdoms, they would surely have first seized South Gaul, and then the weak Christian powers of Italy. Thus Charles Martel was instrumental in determining whether Christianity or Islam prevailed in Europe. It was after the victory at Tours that Charles was first called "martel," or hammer, for the way he dashed his enemies in battle. As a reward for both preventing the Muslim invasion and defending the Roman Church, Charles was appointed to the powerful office of Mayor of the Palace by then Pope Gregory III.

Charles Martel would again come to the pope's aid against the Lombards in Italy, who were taking over papal lands. In a letter written to Charles in 739, Gregory appeals:

Pope Gregory to His Most Excellent Son, Karl, Sub-King

In our great affliction we have thought it necessary to write to you a second time, believing that you are a loving son of St. Peter, the prince of apostles, and of ourselves, and that out of reverence for him you would obey our commands to defend the church of God and his chosen people. We can now no longer endure the persecution of the Lombards, for they have taken from St. Peter all his possessions, even those which were given him by you and your fathers. These Lombards hate and oppress us because we sought protection from you; for the same reason also the church of St. Peter is despoiled and desolated by them. But we have intrusted a more complete account of all our woes to your faithful subject, our present messenger, and he will relate them to you. You, oh son, will receive favor from the same prince of apostles here and in the future life in the presence of God, according as you render speedy aid to his church and to us, that all peoples may recognize the faith and love and singleness of purpose which you display in defending St. Peter and us and his chosen people. For by doing this you will attain lasting fame on earth and eternal life in heaven.

Charles's son Pepin (Pepin the Short) also had a close-knit association with the papacy. In 751, by decree of the pope, he was himself promoted. He went from the inherited rank of Mayor of the Palace—his father's title—to being crowned Pepin III, King of the Franks. According to *The Annals of Lorsch: The Pope Makes the Carolingians Kings:* "[I]n the city of Soissons he was anointed with the holy oil by the hands of Boniface [later Saint Boniface], archbishop and martyr of blessed memory, and was raised to the throne after the custom of the Franks." Pepin's coronation was the beginning of a new relationship between the papacy and the Frankish kings. This would have far-reaching consequences for the Church— especially for the weakening connection between the Roman Church and the Byzantine Empire centered in Constantinople.

Pepin's son Charlemagne would take his family's papal association even further. Shortly after Pope Leo's predecessor, Hadrian I, was installed as pope, the territory that had been given to the papacy by Pepin was invaded by King Desiderius of

Lombardy and seized as part of his own kingdom. This takeover revived an old conflict between the Lombards and the Roman Church. Hadrian then urged Charlemagne to come to his defense. Being loyal to the church, the king of the Franks crossed the Alps with a large army. Charlemagne endured great hardships in climbing the mountain ridges and ragged peaks that had no existing paths or tracks that would have made the journey easier. When he finally entered Italy, he attacked Desiderius' capital of Pavia in 774. The city was eventually taken, Desiderius was banished from Italy for life (Desiderius' son Adalgis was also expelled from Italy), and the kingdom of Lombardy was added to Charlemagne's realm. Following the siege of Pavia, Charlemagne went to Rome to let Pope Hadrian know that the lands stolen by the Lombard king had been restored. Furthermore, he had expanded the Papal States that had been created and donated by his father, Pepin. Because of these acts, Pope Hadrian made Charlemagne protectorate over Italy.

According to Einhard, "Charles . . . went to Rome to set in order the affairs of the Church, which were in great confusion, and passed the whole winter there. It was then that he received the titles of Emperor and Augustus, to which he at first had such an aversion that he declared that he would not have set foot in [Saint Peter's that day], although it was a great feast-day, if he could have foreseen the design of the Pope." However, historians have argued that Charlemagne made this statement after the fact not out of any sense of humility but because being crowned by Leo reestablished the pope's superiority. In fact, Charlemagne had been negotiating for just such a title with the Byzantine government (even though the imperial government in Constantinople was in scandalous disarray). The Byzantines apparently recognized the greatness and strength of the Carolingian empire. So if the pope had not acted when he did, the papacy would have lost its independence to Charlemagne's rule. Therefore, by appointing Charlemagne Roman Emperor, Leo regained his pre-eminence and retained his own power.

Furthermore, what the pope had bestowed he could also withdraw; this made the new emperor indebted to Leo. Being Roman Emperor meant that Charlemagne would have greater authority. Yet at the same time he was now under the authority of the pope, and the alliance between church and state was reinforced—an alliance that would continue in the Christian West.

In fact, the coronation was the culmination of a month of service to the beleaguered pontiff. Leo had been personally appointed by Charlemagne to the papacy when his predecessor, Pope Hadrian I, died. But it was over strenuous objections by the Roman nobility, his fellow church leaders, and the populace as a whole. He subsequently put up with serious accusations of perjury, immorality, and adultery. Then on April 25, 799, during an elaborate procession through the city of Rome, Leo was suddenly attacked by armed men. The pope's attackers— relatives of Hadrian—were carrying out a plot to bring about the new pope's downfall. Leo was beaten mercilessly by the mob. They tried to tear out his eyes and pull out his tongue so that the pope wouldn't be capable of performing his sacred duties—which would mean he would have to resign his office. (According to accounts of the time, his eyes *were* gouged out and his tongue actually cut off, but his injuries miraculously healed. This miracle paved the way for his eventual sainthood.) Leo was then taken to a house where he was to be held for ransom. But a local nobleman, the Duke of Spoleto, helped the pope escape to the monastery of Saint Erasmus to recover from his injuries. When his health was eventually restored, Leo fled from Rome to Paderborn, Germany, seeking protection and help from Charlemagne. Leo argued that given Charlemagne's prestigious position as king of the Franks, he could act as mediator between the two factions. Charlemagne agreed to Leo's appeal. He sent him back to Rome with armed guards and ordered that the pope's accusers assemble to make their charges directly.

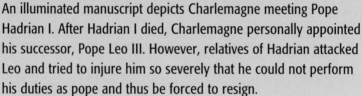

An illuminated manuscript depicts Charlemagne meeting Pope Hadrian I. After Hadrian I died, Charlemagne personally appointed his successor, Pope Leo III. However, relatives of Hadrian attacked Leo and tried to injure him so severely that he could not perform his duties as pope and thus be forced to resign.

On November 24, 800, Charlemagne entered the ancient city in a grand processional with an enormous entourage that included his children. On December 1 he called together a *synod*—a governing council that was comprised of bishops and other church leaders as well as noble Romans—to hear the complaints against the pope. Arguments on both sides were presented. Finally, Leo's accusers agreed that if he denied the allegations against him under oath, the charges would be dropped. Accordingly, the pope swore that all charges were untrue and took an oath of his innocence beside the holy tomb of Saint Peter. The charges were immediately dismissed, and the trial was concluded. However, his accusers were imprisoned when confronted with evidence of their own guilt. With the trial concluded, the path was clear for Charlemagne's coronation as Roman emperor.

The title "emperor" had last been used by Romulus Augustulus, who was overthrown by Odacar the Goth in 476. After that, the power of the Roman Empire, which had been centered, of course, in Rome, passed to the East and the Byzantine Empire, whose capital was Constantinople. The dominion of the Byzantine Empire in theory included Europe. However, in practice, too many small, independent kingdoms under barbarian rule prevented any real unity. Only the pope, who had been made bishop of Rome by the Byzantine Emperor, could claim universal authority in the West. That Charlemagne could claim to be Roman Emperor was a momentous and symbolic event in European history. It was an indicator that Rome had a new heir and a challenger to the Byzantines.

The imperial coronation merely publicly acknowledged the fact that Charlemagne was indeed the supreme ruler of the West. At the same time it made him the ultimate secular protector of Christendom, particularly the Church of Rome. Indeed, Charlemagne often credited his imperial title to an act of God that had been transmitted through the pope. Perhaps to ensure his success as Roman Emperor through God's intervention, Charlemagne made a most generous offering to Saint Peter's Basilica following his coronation. And on the same day that Charlemagne was crowned by the pope, Leo also anointed Charlemagne's son Charles as the new king of the Franks. This ensured for both royals the succession of the dynasty as wearers of the imperial crown. It also ensured for the pope that the papacy would enjoy imperial support and protection.

THE FIRST
CAROLINGIANS
AND THE FRANKS

The legendary Charlemagne was the most famous member of the house of Carolus, which rose to power during the seventh century. The history of the Carolingians is interconnected with the history of the region. Politicians as well as fierce warriors, the first Carolingians paved the way for the exploits of Charlemagne.

Western Civilization had its beginnings in roughly sixth-century France. This was about a century after the fall of the Roman Empire. This, according to Edward Gibbon in his classic *History of the Decline and Fall of the Roman Empire,* occurred in 476 A.D., when the Roman Empire's northernmost outreaches were being overrun by various Germanic tribes:

> The victorious confederates pursued their march, and on the last day of the year, in a season when the waters of the Rhine were most probably frozen, they entered without opposition the defenseless

By the fifth century, the once-mighty Roman Empire was being overrun by various Germanic tribes once dubbed "barbarians" by Julius Caesar himself. This new shift in the balance of power led the way for one group to rise up to fill the power vacuum, and the Franks became the most united group of tribes to set the stage for their domination of Europe.

[sic] provinces of Gaul. This memorable passage of the Suevi, the Vandals, the Alani, and the Burgundians, who never afterwards retreated, may be considered as the fall of the Roman Empire in the countries beyond the Alps; and the

barriers, which had so long separated the savage and the civilized nations of the earth, were from that fatal moment leveled with the ground.

"All Gaul is divided into three parts, one of which the Belgae inhabit, the Aquitani another, the third, those who in their own language are called Celts, and in ours, Gauls. All these differ from each other in language, customs and laws. The river Garonne separates the Gauls from the Aquitani; the Marne and the Seine separate them from the Belgae. . . ."

With these words Julius Caesar began his *Commentaries on the Gallic Wars,* his account of his conquest of Gaul, which lasted from 58–51 B.C. When Caesar marched his legions into Gaul, this land was ruled by the Celts—whom the Romans called *Celtae* or *Galli,* Latin for Gauls. The territory stretched from the western shores of the Mediterranean in the south all the way to the North Sea and from the Atlantic Ocean in the west to the Pyrenees Mountains in the east. The largest and most extensive of the Celtic populations were the Gauls in central and western Europe— the area roughly occupied today by France, Belgium, Luxembourg, and Germany west of the Rhine.

The Gauls were then a scattered alliance of clans; sometimes they functioned independently, and at other times several clans would assemble into one of the region's 400-odd tribes. These tribes, in turn, were often united into nations, 70 or so of which comprised the territory. But for the most part the Gauls lived scattered about the countryside in mud huts, hunting and fishing and farming, and with few towns or cities—a Celtic empire as such never existed. Instead, Gaul was composed of many small tribes that were held together by a common language, art, and culture rather than a common government. Caesar's troops were victorious over the Gauls not only because of their greater numbers, superior weapons, and better discipline and training, but because Gauls often fought among themselves. These tribal rivalries and disunity aided the conquerors to defeat them.

Incorporating Gaul into the Roman Empire began with the census of 27 B.C. Following this population head count and property tally, roads were built, colonies were established at strategic locations, and tax collection was begun. The victorious Caesar understood the importance of good economics when it came to successful empire building. Therefore, he did not destroy the Gallic market towns but instead utilized them to offer Roman goods to his new citizens. The conquered Gauls first purchased imported Roman wine—preferring it to their own beer—and then other Roman products. In turn, Gallic exports included chain mail—which the Celts invented and Roman troops eagerly adopted—and fancy metalwork, foodstuffs, woolen goods, and pottery. The Celts grew accustomed to Roman amenities. They stopped thinking of the Romans as conquerors and began appreciating the fruits of the Roman Empire.

For all of their reputed barbarism, the Gauls were apparently quickly civilized. The historian Strabo, writing only a few years after the conquest, says in his *Geography* that the Gauls "are no longer barbarians" and have been "transformed to the type of the Romans. . . . The people are tilling the country diligently. . . . They provide Rome and Italy with woolen cloaks and salt meat" and "they give heed, for the most part, to the commands of the Romans." Strabo mentions the customs of Druids but says that the Romans put a stop to the practice of human sacrifice and the taking and collecting of heads. In 48 A.D. the Roman Emperor Claudius I (who was, in fact, born at Lyon, France) welcomed Gallic nobles into the Roman Senate. However, at the same time he suppressed Celtic priests and the Druidic religion. He replaced native gods with their Roman counterparts and encouraged the population to worship the emperor as a god himself.

For the next two centuries, Gaul flourished. The Celts enjoyed economic advantages from being part of the Roman Empire. They also benefited from increased security against invasions by the Goths and other barbarian tribes. Scattered mud huts were replaced with villages and towns. The justly celebrated Roman roads and bridges promoted greater trade. Conversely, however, while Gaul flourished, the Roman Empire declined. Rome itself was no longer even the capital of the empire. The capital had officially moved to Constantinople—the old Greek town of Byzantium, renamed by Constantine the Great after himself—the seat of the Eastern Roman (or Byzantine) Empire. As a matter of fact, even before the government officially moved east, emperors had resided in places other than Rome.

By the fifth century, the once-mighty Roman Empire had been severely weakened. This threw Gaul's economy, political unity, and culture into disarray. Many variously sized barbarian tribes migrated through Europe, invading and laying siege to the outreaches of the once-invincible Roman Empire. These conquests splintered Gaul back into separate provinces. Among this accelerated flow of invaders, the most dominant were the Vandals, the Visigoths, the Burgundians, and the Franks. The latter were comprised of the Salians, Chatti, and Ripuarians—relatively insignificant Germanic clans who shared a common language and similar laws. However, only the Franks created a political power that not only outlasted the demise of the Roman Empire but also in effect lives on to this day in the form of Western European civilization.

The actual origin of the Franks is lost to history. But they seem to have been a political confederation of several ancient, small barbarian tribes that had been living in the forests east of the Rhine during the heyday of Roman supremacy. By the end of the second century A.D., the Franks had infiltrated Roman frontier settlements primarily as farmers and soldiers rather than invading warriors. However, they did wage a significant battle against Roman legions in the year 241 around Mainz, located on the Rhine in what is present-day Germany. Though most of the Franks were driven back from the Rhine by the Roman emperor Probus, some Salian Franks managed to cross the river and settle in Gaul. (The area they chose to live is now northern Belgium, where their distinctive Germanic dialect is still spoken.) There, the Salian Franks became peaceful settlers and faithful allies of the Romans—indeed, many volunteered as soldiers in the Imperial Roman Army. As motivation to maintain their peaceful ways, in 358 A.D. Julian the Apostate gave them the region of Toxandria (Belgium), which lay between the Meuse and Scheldt Rivers.

The Salian Franks were comprised of several dynastic tribes led by individual chiefs. The most successful of these tribes was the Merovingians (431–751). It derived its name from its chieftain leader, Merovech, or Merowen. Known for their flowing shoulder-length hair—other Frankish warriors shaved the backs of their heads—the Merovingians were especially successful in extending the Salian dominion southward.

The founder of the Frankish kingdom was Clovis (465–511), the grandson of Merovech. He succeeded to the throne when he was only 15 and ruled until his death in 511. The Frankish impact on Western Europe dates from Clovis' accession as king. He unified the Franks under the Merovingian dynasty and finally ended Roman rule in northern Gaul when he defeated the Roman forces at Soissons in 486. He then subjugated the Alamanni in 496 and overthrew the Visigoths in Aquitaine. The Burgundians were also defeated—though apparently without any lasting ill will, since Clovis married Clotilda, niece of the King of Burgundy. He thus completed the conquest that had been begun by his grandfather and extended Frankish rule to the

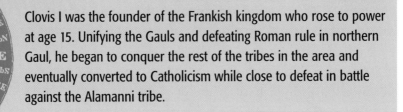

Clovis I was the founder of the Frankish kingdom who rose to power at age 15. Unifying the Gauls and defeating Roman rule in northern Gaul, he began to conquer the rest of the tribes in the area and eventually converted to Catholicism while close to defeat in battle against the Alamanni tribe.

whole southern region as far as the Pyrenees.

According to Gregory, Bishop of Tours—writing about a century after the fact and skewing his account from the viewpoint of a church leader—it was around this time that Clovis converted to Catholic Christianity, following Clotilde's pleas to do so. Clovis, being king (and, not incidentally, comparing himself to the Emperor Constantine, who had also embraced Christianity), decreed that his people should also convert to Christianity. From the *Medieval Sourcebook,* Gregory recounts:

> The queen unceasingly urged the king to acknowledge the true God and forsake idols. But he could not in any wise be brought to believe until a war broke out with the Alamanni. Then he was by necessity compelled to confess what he had before willfully denied.
>
> It happened that the two armies were in battle, and there was a great slaughter. Clovis' army was near to utter destruction. . . . [He] raised his eyes to heaven, saying, "Jesus Christ, whom Clotilde declares to be the son of the living God, . . . I beseech the glory of thy aid. If thou shalt grant me victory over these enemies, . . . I will believe in thee and be baptized in thy name. . . ."
>
> When he had said these things, the Alamanni turned their backs and began to flee. When they saw that their king was killed, they submitted to the sway of Clovis, saying: "We wish that no more people should perish. Now we are thine." When the king had forbidden further war and praised his soldiers, he told the queen how he had won the victory by calling on the name of Christ. . . .
>
> [Clovis then] ordered the [baptismal] font to be prepared. . . . Then the king . . . was baptized . . . and was anointed with the sacred chrism with the sign of the cross of Christ. Of his army there were baptized more than three thousand.

Clovis' conversion was more than just a personal choice; becoming a Christian ensured his political success. Whether he was merely politically savvy or truly believed in the tenets of the Church, Clovis converted to orthodox Roman Christianity. By contrast, the other Germanic kings converted to Arianism. This form of Christian belief was considered by Church fathers to be heretical because it holds that God is the only divinity and denies the divinity of the Trinity. Clovis' conversion to established orthodox Catholicism was rewarded with the support of the powerful Catholic hierarchy of Gaul and Rome. It also made Clovis' Frankish rule more palatable to the conquered Roman Catholic population of Gaul. Thus by this one act Clovis helped assure his status as King of the Franks.

When Clovis died in 511, the kingdom of the Franks was divided among his four sons. This was predetermined under the Frankish law of inheritance. The kingdom itself was considered the king's own property—the "royal domains," which is to say, the wealth of the king. Not surprisingly, parceling out the kingdom equally among the king's sons was the Merovingians' greatest disadvantage in maintaining a unified kingdom. It also wreaked havoc on the family itself. According to historian Peter Lasko in *The Kingdom of the Franks*:

> The second son, Clodmir, died in 524, and the others murdered his children in order to divide his share among themselves. The eldest, Theodoric, died in 534 and his only surviving grandson in 555. The third, Childebert, died in 558, leaving the youngest, Chlotar I, in possession of the whole kingdom. His own son rebelled against him—"like Absolom" says Gregory of Tours—but Chlotar defeated him, shut him up in a hut with his wife and family, and burned them all to death, an action for which he later seems to have felt no little remorse.

CLOTAIRE·I·ROY·DE·FRANCE·
VII·
Tiré du Cabinet du Roy par les
mains du S^r. d'Oye

Chlotar I was the son of Clovis I and assumed power after his older brothers died. However, his reign was marked by internal power struggles—even his own son ended up rebelling against him. Chlotar in turn had his son and his family burned to death.

When Clovis' kingdom was split four ways, four new political units were created: the kingdoms of Reims, Soissons, Orléans, and Paris. As his sons died in turn, further divisions were made. Austrasia was partitioned off from Reims, Burgundy from Orléans, and Neustria from Soissons. Aside from the family feuds (and the occasional murder) over political power, these increasingly subdivided holdings undermined the strength of the Frankish empire by making its frontiers vulnerable to raids.

While Clovis' descendants were busy fighting bitter civil wars, the noble landowners in the kingdom were whittling away at the waning royal authority. With trade and agriculture in disarray and the land increasingly subdivided, these noblemen assumed both civil (administrative, legal, and tax) and military power. By the middle of the seventh century, they were essentially running the kingdom. The last Merovingian king who exhibited any authority had been Dagobert, who ascended the throne in 629. But, as Peter Lasko says, "even he, an unusually strong personality among the later Merovingian kings, was able to stem the flow against the Frankish royal house only for a time. The growing antagonism of the aristocracy—Dagobert complained that the nobles had robbed him of the best estates and domains in his kingdom—was too strong for the king to resist." By 640 the Merovingian dynasty that Clovis I had established was essentially powerless. The last Merovingian kings were mere children when crowned and only lived until their 20s. Though they figuratively sat on the throne, they actually lived on luxurious country estates, "exercising no influence on the course of events" and being little more than figureheads.

The Merovingian family is commonly thought to have lasted until the time of Childeric III, who ruled from 743 until

752. He was then deposed and thrown into a cloister at the decree of the pontiff, Pope Stephen. However, as Charlemagne's personal biographer Einhard relates:

> [A]lthough to all outward appearance [the Merovingian dynasty] ended with [Childeric], it had long since been devoid of vital strength, and conspicuous only from bearing the empty epithet *Royal;* the real power and authority in the kingdom lay in the hands of the chief officer of the court, the so-called Mayor of the Palace. . . . The Mayor of the Palace took charge of the government and of everything that had to be planned or executed at home or abroad.

By the beginning of the seventh century, the office of Mayor of the Palace had become a hereditary one. At around that time, the position was held by the head of the Arnulfing family (later known as the Carolingians), Pepin II of Heristal, who was Charlemagne's great-grandfather. Carolingians were now ruling the Frankish government as kings in everything but name. When Pepin died in 714, his two older legitimate sons had already died as well. So the title passed to his illegitimate son, Charles. (Though he was Pepin's illegitimate son, he was not excluded from the succession.) The only other contender for the position of Mayor of the Palace was Pepin's six-year-old grandson, Theodoald—who was himself illegitimate. The boy's grandmother naturally wanted her own lineage to have the power, and she had Charles thrown in prison and assumed guardianship of Theodoald. But Charles escaped and put himself in charge.

Charles Martel was born around 688. Considered the founder of the Carolingian dynasty, Charles was a military genius as well as a very capable ruler. He consolidated control over the outlying regions of the kingdom and extended the boundaries to the east. By the time his campaigns were completed, he had re-established the territory of the Frankish Empire, including the lands that had been lost over the years. Charles Martel was also a smart politician. He distributed lands owned by the church among his retainers so that they would support his military actions. This also further linked the church and the state, which continue through Charlemagne's reign, down through the centuries.

But a new threat was on the horizon at the outermost reaches of his kingdom, originating over the border in Spain. In 732 an immense army of Saracens trekked over the Pyrenees and invaded Gaul. Driven out to Spain in 721 by Eudes, the Duke of Aquitaine, the Muslims had returned in 725. They got as far as Burgundy, where they destroyed the town of Autun. The duke was unable to resist the Muslims and negotiated with them, giving his daughter in marriage to one of their chiefs. Once again the Saracens were intent on conquering Gaul. Led by the governor of Spain, Abd-er-Rahman, this Muslim invasion force overwhelmed the defending Christian troops of Duke Eudes. They advanced as far as the Loire, pillaging and burning as they went. In October 732 Charles Martel gathered an army together and went to do battle against Abd-er-Rahman. For a week the two encamped armies faced each other at the point where the Vienne and Clain Rivers meet, near the town of Poitiers. The battle was swift and decisive, and Charles Martel emerged the victor. The vanquished Muslims retreated back to Spain.

The Battle of Poitiers is considered one of the most important in the history of Europe. The outcome determined whether Christianity or Islam would prevail throughout Europe. According to the *Chronicle of Saint Denis*:

The Muslims planned to go to Tours to destroy the Church of St. Martin, the city, and the whole country. Then came against them the Glorious Prince Charles, at the head of his whole force. He drew up his host, and he fought as fiercely as the hungry wolf falls upon the stag. By the grace of Our Lord, he wrought a great slaughter upon the enemies of Christian faith, so that—as history bears witness—he slew in that battle 300,000 men, likewise their king by name Abderrahman. Then was [Charles] first called "Martel," or as a hammer of iron, of steel, and of every other metal, even so he dashed: and smote in the battle all his enemies. . . .

After many other small battles, in which numerous rebellions were suppressed, Charles Martel died in 741. He was buried in the abbey of Saint-Denis near Paris. This would be the resting place of many later French kings.

Charles Martel's two sons—Pepin the Short and his older brother Carloman—succeeded him, reigning jointly. But their sovereignty wasn't without resistance. Their father's illegitimate son, Griffon, claimed the right to share in their rule—as had the illegitimate Charles Martel himself. Plus the dukes of Aquitaine and Alamanni both battled to rid themselves of their Frankish overlords, and the Saxons and Bavarians fought for independence as well. But the two brothers were victorious, and the kingdom of the Franks was reunified.

In 747, Carloman—in the words of Charlemagne's biographer, Einhard—"renounced the heavy cares of an earthly crown and retired to Rome. Here he exchanged his worldly garb for a cowl and built a monastery on Mt. Oreste . . . " With Carloman now a monk, Pepin was left as sole ruler. This consolidated Pepin's power and worked to unite the kingdom. It was also at this point that the king in all but name—his official title was still Mayor of the Palace—

sought to be legally called "king." As Einhard states of Childric III, the Merovingian king who still officially ruled:

> There was nothing left the King to do but to be content with his name of King, his flowing hair, and long beard, to sit on his throne and play the ruler, to give ear to the ambassadors that came from all quarters, and to dismiss them, as if on his own responsibility, in words that were in fact suggested to him, or even imposed upon him. He had nothing that he could call his own beyond this vain title of King and the precarious support allowed by the Mayor of the Palace in his discretion, except a single country seat that brought him but a very small income. There was a dwelling house upon this, and a small number of servants attached to it, sufficient to perform the necessary offices.

Einhard's account conveys the contrast between the dishonored status of the king and the exalted and powerful status of the Mayor of the Palace. Therefore, it stood to reason that in 751, Pepin and the Frankish nobles discussed whether he could morally and legally assume the crown. It was decided to appeal for a solution to Pope Zachary since the pope was recognized by all as the custodian and interpreter of the moral law. The pontiff replied that *"ut melius esset. Illum regem vocari, qui potestatem haberes, quam illum qui sine regali potestate maneret"* ["better for him to be called the king who holds the power than the one who remains (king in name) without the regal power"]. Reassured by this decision, Pepin had himself proclaimed king at Soissons in 752. Two years later, the sitting pope, Stephen III, traveled across the Alps from Rome. On July 28, 754, the house of Arnulf (the Carolingians' family name) was, by a solemn act of Holy See, established on the throne that until then had been nominally occupied by the house of Merowig (the Merovingians). Not only Pepin was anointed with the oil of kingship by the Church, but his sons Charles and Carloman were as well. The last Merovingian king, Childeric III, was sent to a cloister to end his days.

After having wielded sovereign power almost without interruption for over a century, the Carolingians finally got to actually rule from the Frankish throne in their name. And because the pope had thrown the moral support of the Church behind Pepin, the Frankish kingdom was essentially bestowed on the Carolingian family. This in turn increased the Church's importance because of its strong ties to the dynasty.

Pepin ruled over the Franks from 752 to 768, when he died of dropsy in Paris. Several days before he died, Pepin—following the tradition of Frankish law—divided up the kingdom equally between his two sons, the older Charles (later Charles the Great, or Charlemagne) and Carloman. Pepin died on September 24, 768. Like his father, he was buried at Saint-Denis.

Pepin the Short had divided his kingdom equally between the two brothers, but in a practical sense the division was hardly equal. Charles was given the outlying regions of the realm, which were far more prone to rebellion; his younger brother was given the more stable and settled interior provinces. The regions held by Charlemagne surrounded his younger brother's on two sides. However, their father had distributed them so as to stem any conflicts that might arise out of national fervor by their various subjects. This was particularly true in the former German dependencies, whose populations had only recently been won over to Christianity.

Nonetheless, despite this seemingly rational division of territory, the brothers soon fell out with one another. Hunald, the former Duke of Aquitaine who had been defeated by Pepin 20 years before, left the cloister where he had been living as a monk to stir up a revolt in his former realm. Aquitaine was mostly under Charlemagne's rule, and Carloman should have come to his brother's aid. Instead, he

Pepin the Short was the son of Charles Martel. After his brother Carloman became a monk, Pepin assumed power, although he was not legally the "king"—this position was held by Childeric III, the Merovingian king who officially ruled but in essence was a figurehead. After seeking Pope Zachary's advice, Pepin had himself proclaimed king in 752.

maintained that since *his* dominion wasn't affected by the revolt, it was none of his business. Despite his brother's lack of support, Charlemagne vanquished Hunald, who was eventually stoned to death for breaking his vows as a monk.

Carloman died soon after these events—in December 771, just three years into his joint reign. A letter purported to be from "Monk Cathwulph" to Charlemagne recounts the reasons why the king should have been grateful for this turn of events, among them being: "Third . . . God has preserved you from the wiles of your brother. . . . Fifth, and not the least, that God has removed your brother from this earthly kingdom." It wasn't recorded for posterity whether Charlemagne agreed with this assessment. Nonetheless, Charlemagne quickly grabbed possession of his brother's lands, dispossessing his two nephews and sister-in-law. (They fled to the protection of the King of Lombardy.) Charlemagne now sat on the Frankish throne alone.

A MAN
APART

Charlemagne was 29 when he became sole king. It was a role he had been preparing for virtually all of his life. Having been anointed to kingly office when he was just 10 years old, Charlemagne was still a child when he repeatedly accompanied his father into battle. Such early experiences developed his military skills. This military prowess together with his unusual physical strength and nationalistic pride made him a popular hero to his subjects long before he became their king.

But who was the *real* Charles the Great, the legendary Charlemagne? As is frequently the case with charismatic men of greatness, Charlemagne was a complex and often contradictory human being.

The man considered by most historians to be the greatest of medieval kings was born on April 2, 742, according to most accounts. His exact place of birth remains in doubt, though it is believed to be Aachen in modern-day Germany and what was then Aix-la-Chapelle,

Charlemagne was the older son of Pepin the Short. He became king at age 29, and his regal presence was only enhanced by his sheer physical stature—standing 6'4", which was extremely tall for average human beings in the eighth century. He also preferred to wear humbler clothing than was normal for rulers of the time.

France. Regardless of the exact date and place of his birth, Charles, later known as Charlemagne, seems to have been destined for greatness from the start.

Charlemagne was the older son of Pepin (also known as Pipin) the Short and Berthrada (or Bertha), daughter of the Count of Laon. Pepin and Berthrada may or may not have been legally married at the time of their son's birth. As a boy, Charlemagne enjoyed riding and hunting and training in the use of weapons. He also practiced the Christian religion and took an interest in singing. As an adult, he stood out like a towering pine tree among his fellow Celts, being six feet four inches. Teutonic in appearance—he was of German blood— he had long, fair hair and was clean shaven (many paintings and drawings of Charlemagne erroneously depict him wearing a beard), though he may have worn a mustache at times. His biographer Einhard described his nose as "powerful" and noted that although he had a short, thick neck and a prominent belly, "the symmetry of the rest of his body concealed these defects." Apparently, for all his size, his voice was rather high pitched and thin.

According to Einhard, Charlemagne was a man of restrained and frugal habits. However, he made good use of his time, and today he would likely be called skilled at multitasking:

> Charles was temperate in eating, and particularly so in drinking, for he abominated drunkenness in anybody, much more in himself and those of his household; but he could not easily abstain from food, and often complained that fasts injured his health. He very rarely gave entertainments, only on great feast days, and then to large numbers of people. His meals ordinarily consisted of four courses, not counting the roast, which his huntsmen used to bring in on the spit; he was more fond of this than of any other dish. While at table, he listened to reading or music [rather than being entertained by traditional jesters]. The subjects of the readings were the stories and deeds of olden time: he was fond, too, of St. Augustine's books, and especially of the one entitled *The City of God.*
>
> He was so moderate in the use of wine and all sorts of drink that he rarely allowed himself more than three cups in the course of a meal. In summer after the midday meal, he would eat some fruit, drain a single cup, put off his clothes and shoes, just as he did for the night, and rest for two or three hours. He was in the habit of awaking and

rising from bed four or five times during the night. While he was dressing and putting on his shoes, he not only gave audience to his friends, but if the Count of the Palace told him of any suit in which his judgment was necessary, he had the parties brought before him forthwith, took cognizance of the case, and gave his decision, just as if he were sitting on the judgment-seat. This was not the only business that he transacted at this time, but he performed any duty of the day whatever, whether he had to attend to the matter himself or to give commands concerning it to his officers.

Charlemagne understood the importance of learning. This was something his parents had instilled in him, who saw to it that all of their children (including their daughter, Gisela, who later entered a nunnery) were educated. They had all been taught to read and speak Latin—Charlemagne spoke it "as well as his native tongue"—Greek, and French.

Charlemagne in turn saw to it that his own children were well schooled. According to Einhard, "The plan that he adopted for his children's education was . . . to have both boys and girls instructed in the liberal arts, to which he also turned his own attention." And it wasn't just his own children who benefited from Charlemagne's appreciation of education. He promoted learning among all of his subjects and believed that education was an essential element of Frankish life. In fact, he himself studied "zealously." He brought to his palace Peter of Pisa to teach him grammar and Albin Alcuin, a monk from Britain, considered the greatest scholar of the day. Alcuin was persuaded by Charlemagne to come to Aachen to design a curriculum for the palace school. The course of study that Alcuin developed is, in fact, the basis for the seven liberal arts and included mathematics, music, astronomy, and classical literature.

Apparently the king was extremely interested in learning

Charlemagne regarded education highly, promoting it among his subjects and having a love of learning himself. In fact, he would often read while eating instead of being entertained by a court jester. Here he is seen visiting with young students.

about all manner of things and could converse at length on many subjects. Recounts Einhard in *The Life of Charlemagne*:

> He was so eloquent, indeed, that he might have passed for a teacher of eloquence. He most zealously cultivated the liberal arts, held those who taught them in great esteem, and conferred great honors upon them. . . . The King spent much

time and labor . . . studying logic [how to think], rhetoric [how to speak], dialectics, and especially astronomy; he learned to reckon [by the stars] and used to investigate the motions of the heavenly bodies most curiously, with an intelligent scrutiny.

Yet, ironically, although Charlemagne could read with ease, he never mastered writing. Says Einhard, "He . . . tried to write, and used to keep tablets and blanks in bed under his pillow that at leisure hours he might accustom his hand to form the letters; however, as he did not begin his efforts . . . [until] late in life, they met with ill success." Despite this inability, he attempted to produce a book of German grammar. He also had a collection of ancient folk songs and tales of folk heroes compiled. Unfortunately this compilation "ceased to be appreciated" and was later lost.

Charlemagne was a walking contradiction in his personal life. Though a devout Christian and devoted to the Church, he nonetheless had at least four—possibly five—lawful wives and four or five concubines. He had children by all but two of his spouses (legal or otherwise). Accounts vary as to their number—either 16 or 18 in all. (Einhard writes that only three of Charlemagne's children died before him; however, other historical accounts maintain that at least 10 offspring died before their father.)

Some reports of Charlemagne's life say that his first legal wife was Himiltrude, whom he supposedly married around 768. (Einhard, however, designates her as Charlemagne's concubine.) They had one son, Pepin the Hunchback. (Pepin would later plot with several nobles who—as Einhard tells it—"seduced him with vain promises of the royal authority. When his deceit was discovered, and the conspirators were punished, his head was shaved, and he was suffered, in accordance with his wishes, to devote himself to a religious life in the monastery of Prüm.")

When Charlemagne and Himiltrude divorced, she encouraged

him to remarry because their son was deformed. At this point Charlemagne's mother insisted that as a smart political alliance, her son should marry Desideria, a daughter of Desiderius, King of the Lombards. He did so in 771, but after only a year, he renounced Desideria, probably because she didn't bear him any children. At the end of that same year, he married Hildegarde of Swabia, "a woman of high birth." Charlemagne had at least seven children with Hildegarde (including Charles the Younger, King of France; Pepin I, King of Italy; and Louis I, King of France, Germany, and Italy). He stayed married to her until her death in 783.

Wasting no time after this wife's death, Charlemagne married Fastrada that same year. They had two daughters, one of whom became an abbess. At Fastrada's death, the king married his last and favorite wife, Luitgard. They had one daughter, who also became an abbess. Luitgard died in 800, and from that time until his own death, Charlemagne had three more concubines: Gersuinda, a Saxon by whom he had a daughter; Regina, the mother of two sons; and Ethelind (also called Adalind), with whom he had at least one other son, possibly two. Some historical accounts add yet another wife or mistress, Madelgard, between Luitgard and Gersuinda.

Perhaps not surprisingly, Church officials turned a blind eye to Charlemagne's lax morals. He was, after all, the head of an empire that encompassed most of Western Europe. He also fought tirelessly as defender of the faith against invading heathens. In fact, when negotiating with Islamic rulers, he demanded fair treatment of their Christian population. He also donated vast sums of money, as well as land, to the Church, heaping its treasure "with a vast wealth of gold, silver, and precious stones." He also was exceedingly generous to the popes and even "sent money to distressed Christians in foreign lands."

Yet, in contradiction to his kindness and generosity, his piety could turn ruthless and cruel when it came to his determination to spread Christianity among the heathens. His laws issued to his conquered subjects were often shortsighted and cruel. Charlemagne triumphed over the Saxons after a bloody struggle that lasted 30 years (772–804). The Saxons were the last German tribe that persisted in worshipping pagan gods, so Charlemagne was also determined to convert them to Christianity.

The Saxon wars have been called religious wars—the assertion being that Charlemagne converted the Saxons by force. The Church claimed that Charlemagne intended mainly to punish the Saxons for their repeated raids into the Frankish kingdom, where they "burned churches and monasteries, killed priests, and sacrificed their prisoners of war to the gods." But Charlemagne issued laws that decreed the death penalty for all Saxons who failed to be baptized and celebrate Christian festivals or who cremated their dead in the pagan tradition. In 782, the king issued the uncompromising "Capitulation de partibus Saxoniae"—the same year he executed 4,500 Saxons at Verdun.

Charlemagne maintained warm friendships with his fellow nobles. At one gathering, according to Hincmar, Archbishop of Reims, Charlemagne could be seen "saluting the men of most note, conversing with those whom he seldom saw, showing a tender interest toward the elders, and disporting himself with the young."

By all accounts he was a close and loving father to his children. He apparently cherished their company. Says Einhard in *The Life of Charlemagne:*

> He was so careful of the training of his sons and daughters that he never took his meals without them when he was at home and never made a journey without them; his sons would ride at his side, and his daughters follow him, while a number of his bodyguard, detailed for their protection, brought up the rear.

Apparently, though, his attachment ran a little too deeply when it came to his daughters. Charlemagne was unwilling to

Berthrada, Charlemagne's beloved mother, died in 783. While a devoted son and father to his children, he actually forbade his daughters from marriage.

allow these beautiful young women to marry—either "to a man of their own nation or to a foreigner"—and kept them by his side until his death, insisting that "he could not dispense with their society." Though adultery went against Church teachings, Charlemagne readily acknowledged the fact that his daughters had illicit love affairs; these resulted in several illegitimate grandchildren running around the palace. Charlemagne willingly accepted these accidents of birth—especially given his own history. (In Einhard's carefully worded language, "Though otherwise happy, he experienced the malignity of fortune as far as they were concerned; yet he concealed his knowledge of the rumors current in regard to them, and of the suspicions entertained of their honor.")

Charlemagne was equally devoted to his mother, Queen Dowager Berthrada, and "entertained the greatest veneration for her." Berthrada lived with her son until her death on July 12, 783. Charlemagne buried her "with great pomp" in the Basilica of Saint-Denis, alongside her late husband, Pepin. The king's sister, Abbess Gisela, had devoted herself to religious life from her girlhood. But Charlemagne felt as much affection for her as for his mother. The same was true of his grandchildren. When his son, Pepin I, King of Italy, died, leaving a son and two daughters, Charlemagne appointed his grandson to replace Pepin on the throne and raised his granddaughters with his own daughters.

The palace at Aix-la-Chapelle was apparently quite a lively, happy place. When learning wasn't being stressed, physical activities were. Charlemagne loved to hunt and ride horses. He especially loved to swim—so much so that he had a swimming pool built at the palace there—and he was evidently so adept that no one could surpass him. According to Einhard, "He used not only to invite his sons to his bath, but his nobles and friends, and now and then a troop of his retinue or body guard so that a hundred or more persons sometimes bathed with him."

Charlemagne was dedicated to learning. He was an innovative administrator. His religious convictions were the catalyst for Christianizing Europe. And he was devoted to his family. Yet it is as a warrior that he is perhaps best remembered—in legend and in history.

THE
WARRIOR
KING

"**B**y the sword and the cross," Charlemagne became master of Western Europe. When he became sole king in 771, he immediately put into practice two plans of action. One was to unite all the Germanic peoples into one kingdom, which meant expanding the Frankish borders to include other regions. The other was to convert his entire kingdom to Christianity. These two goals meant that for virtually the whole of his reign Charlemagne was occupied with warfare.

Yet despite his many military triumphs, Charlemagne cannot really be called a distinguished general. He essentially inherited the highly trained army of his grandfather and father before him. However, the king had two qualities that aided his continued military success: He was a dogged campaigner and could often wear down his enemies through sheer force. And he was a fierce warrior.

Charlemagne's first military undertaking on his own after his father's death was the Aquitanian War, which had been started by

This depiction of Charlemagne's forces illustrated how often the king was involved in one conflict or another. This was necessary in order for him to achieve his goals of uniting the Germanic tribes and converting his kingdom to Christianity. Indeed, his war with the Saxons lasted over 30 years.

Pepin and hadn't yet concluded. Believing it could be quickly brought to a close, Charlemagne called on his brother, Carloman, to aid him in the campaign. His brother withheld his support, but Charlemagne nonetheless was victorious. "[B]y his patience and firmness he . . . completely gained his ends," says the king's biographer, Einhard, in his *Life of Charlemagne*.

After bringing the war in Aquitania to a successful close,

Charlemagne was once again preparing to go into battle. In 773 he was called on by Pope Hadrian I to help him wage war on the Lombards.

The Lombards had established their own kingdom in Italy late in the sixth century. They later confiscated lands that belonged to the Roman Church. Charlemagne's father, Pepin, had previously undertaken the mission of getting back papal lands at the urging of the pope. But Pepin didn't have much support from his fellow nobles at that time. Still, he had been successful, and the campaign had been quickly concluded.

Yet again, though, the Lombards were up to their old ways: seizing the lands that belonged to the papacy. (Some historians speculate that King Desiderius actually waged the war because Charlemagne had divorced the king's sister after being married for only a year. He sent her away, claiming the marriage was not valid. This had infuriated Desiderius, who vowed to get even with Charlemagne.) But this time, the campaign against them would differ in both difficulty and results. Charlemagne and his men had to cross over the Alps into Italy. The mountains were trackless and the peaks ragged, which made for a grueling journey. Charlemagne marched into Pavia, the Lombard capital. After laying siege to the city, Charlemagne defeated King Desiderius at the Battle of Pavia, capturing the king, who was forced to join a monastery. The Lombard ruler's son and heir, Adalgis, was sent into exile from Italy.

But of all the wars that Charlemagne waged, none was fought for so long, so bitterly, and at such a great cost as the war against the pagan Saxons. The conflict began as early as 772 and continued for 33 consecutive years. Charlemagne "took the field" against them at least 18 times during those years. His first attempt to conquer the Saxons was partly in retribution for their attacks on the lower Rhine region—but it was equally for their pagan religion.

The Saxons worshipped the ancient gods of Valhalla. They would gather to offer a sacrifice—sometimes human—to

Irminsul, the sacred tree that stood at Eresburg. At that time the people of Saxony (today's northwestern Germany and parts of the Netherlands) were still slaying Christian missionaries. Their British kinsmen, on the other hand, were dedicated Christians who were erecting massive cathedrals. Charlemagne couldn't tolerate the ways of the German Saxons, and in July 772 he made his first military foray into their country. He stormed Eresburg, destroyed a sacred temple, and burned the sacred tree of Irminsul.

From 775 on Charlemagne's primary purpose in subduing the Saxons was to convert them to Christianity and assimilate the region into his kingdom. (Reports Einhard, "[T]he Saxons, like almost all Germans, were a ferocious folk, given to the worship of devils, hostile to our Faith, and they did not consider it dishonorable to transgress and violate all law—be it human or divine.")

For a while it seemed that the campaigns had worked. Many Saxon noblemen declared their allegiance to Charlemagne, and between 775 and 777 mass baptisms were carried out. The Eastphalians were the first to convert, followed by the Engrians, and lastly the Westphalians. By 776 fully three-quarters of Saxony had declared loyalty to Charlemagne. Furthermore, in 777 an assembly of officials gathered in Paderborn that "sealed the submission of the Saxons." But, in fact, the Saxons were neither ready to yield to their old enemy nor willing to give up their paganism. As Einhard recounts:

> It is hard to say how often they were conquered [Charlemagne actually waged war against the Saxons at least 18 times] and, humbly submitting to the King, promised to do what was enjoined upon them.... They were sometimes so much weakened and reduced that they promised to renounce the worship of devils and to adopt Christianity, but they were no less ready to violate these terms than prompt to accept them so that it is impossible to tell which came easier to them to do.

Charlemagne had published a Saxon code of law. He even let some of the Saxon chieftains—many of whom had been baptized—maintain their power. But after two years had passed, and the king was busy waging war elsewhere, the northern tribes rose up against their conqueror. They killed Christian priests and missionaries, rebuilt their temples, and repeatedly crossed the border into the Frankish kingdom to kill and pillage there as well. Charlemagne was furious. In 783 he decreed that the Saxons had violated their treaty of allegiance, and had ignored the baptisms they had undergone, thus committing high treason, an even worse offense. He rounded up the leaders of the revolt—some 4,500 Saxons—and slaughtered them. This became known as the Massacre of Verdun. Despite this retribution, the Saxons continued sporadic skirmishing. In 792 Charlemagne deported many Saxon citizens, replacing them with loyal Franks. Even this did not stop the Saxons from fighting. The last Saxons weren't vanquished until 804.

In 777, in the middle of the almost continual struggle against the Saxons, Charlemagne went off to fight a battle on another front. Although it was a minor campaign, it would become his most famous—and the one that would hand him his biggest defeat.

Spain had seen the arrival of the powerful Muslim chief Abd-er-Rahman, who established himself as the Caliph of Cordoba. His ruthlessness and cruelty didn't sit well with his subjects, who conspired to get rid of him. Three chieftains in particular hated the caliph so much that they made an unprecedented move. These Moorish leaders decided to seek the help of the mighty Christian leader in their uprising against the emir. Al-Arabi, governor of Barcelona, Abd-er-Rahman ibn Habib, and Abu 'l-Aswad sought out Charlemagne at the Paderborn assembly while it deliberated the fate of the Saxons.

Believing that the Saxons were no longer a threat, Charlemagne agreed to take on the mission. He marched as many men as he could muster over the Pyrenees into Spain. The plan was to lay siege to the city of Sargossa in north-central Spain. According to Einhard, the campaign was successful—"All the towns and castles that he attacked surrendered."

Charlemagne's forces on their Spanish campaign actually went to aid other Moorish leaders who sought Charlemagne's help in ousting their emir, Abd-er-Rahman. His forces were successful in besieging Sargossa and all the towns and cities in their path, but soon the Saxons would require Charlemagne's attention once more.

Then word came that the Saxons, taking advantage of absence of the Frankish army, were once again ravaging the realm. Charlemagne immediately set off back to his kingdom.

But the return trip in 778 proved disastrous. The rear guard of Charlemagne's army was attacked by Basques—or the "Gascons" as Einhard called them—who previously had declared themselves to be faithful subjects of the king. But the Basque leader had called together all the mountaineers who acknowledged him as their chief, and they laid in wait in the high mountain pass of Roncesvalles. When the Franks began their return journey home, the main body of the troops met with no difficulty and had no hint of danger. But the rear guard, which was considerably behind and encumbered with its plunder, was overwhelmed by the mountaineers. Every man was slain. Some of the bravest of Charlemagne's commanders perished on this occasion. One of these chief officers was Roland, or Orlando, Governor of the March of Brittany. His name and the manner of his death later became famous in the celebrated medieval epic *The Song of Roland (Chanson de Roland)*. This was the first and unquestionably the greatest of the *chansons de geste*, or songs of deeds.

According to Einhard, the attackers had the advantage in several ways:

[T]he Gascons, who lay in ambush on the top of a very high mountain, attacked the rear of the baggage train and the rear guard in charge of it and hurled them down to the very bottom of the valley [at Roncevalles]. In the struggle that ensued, they cut them off to a man; they then plundered the baggage and dispersed with all speed in every direction under cover of approaching night. The lightness of their armor and the nature of the battle ground stood the Gascons in good stead on this occasion, whereas the Franks fought at a disadvantage in every respect because of the weight of their armor and the unevenness of the ground. Einhard, the king's steward; Anselm, Count Palatine; and Roland, Governor of the March of Brittany, with so many others, fell in this engagement. This ill turn could not be avenged for the nonce because the enemy scattered so widely after carrying out their plan that not the lease clue could be had to their whereabouts.

Roland (or Orlando as he is sometimes called) was one of Charlemagne's officers who died in the mountain pass of Roncesvalles. Attacked by Basques, all were slain, and Roland's death was celebrated in the medieval epic poem *Chanson de Roland*, or *The Song of Roland*.

This defeat was an unusual occurrence in Charlemagne's military career. It also marks the end of the period of major expansion during the king's rule.

Although Bavaria maintained its independence, it was technically part of the Frankish kingdom. This meant that Duke Tassilo III of Bavaria owed his loyalty to Charlemagne. But the duke was married to a daughter of the deposed

Lombard king Desiderius, whom Charlemagne had banished years before. To please his wife, the duke entered into a treaty with the Huns, who bordered Bavaria to the east. A brief war was fought, and Charlemagne won. According to Einhard, "Tassilo did not think that it was for his own or his people's good to persist, so he surrendered himself to the king . . . and promised by oath not to give ear to anyone who should attempt to turn him from his allegiance. So this war, which bade fair to be very grievous, came very quickly to an end." Bavaria— whose subjects were Christians—was now completely incorporated into Charlemagne's realm.

Charlemagne made Ratisbon the residence of the Bavarian dukes. From this base he staged campaigns against the Avars, or Huns. (Avar is present-day Hungary and Austria.) In 791, Charlemagne fought "virtually the entire Avar nation in battle." Except for the war against the Saxons, it was, says Einhard, "the greatest that he waged; he took it up with more spirit than any of his other wars. . . ."

At the start of the war against the Avars, Charlemagne himself headed up his forces. He subsequently entrusted the campaigns to his son Pepin, governors of the provinces, nobles, and even lieutenants. One province, Pannonia, had its population completely wiped out. After so many battles over the years, the Khan's palace there showed no trace of human habitation.

The Avars were so completely vanquished that they essentially vanished as a tribe. As Einhard recorded: "The entire body of the Hun nobility perished in this contest—and all its glory with it." What didn't vanish were the country's riches. The Franks came away from the war with riches beyond any booty gotten in the past. Einhard justifies the taking of this "valuable spoil" by asserting that "one may well think that the Franks took justly from the Huns what the Huns had formerly taken unjustly from other nations."

Conflict between the king of Denmark and the king of the Franks was probably inevitable. Hostility between the two realms had existed for decades. It stemmed from the eastward expansion of the Frankish empire, which threatened the independence of Denmark. The Danes also felt threatened by the many Christian missionaries making their way throughout the country. After Charlemagne defeated the Saxons in 785, the Frankish Empire stretched all the way to the Danish Empire in the north, incorporating Frisia (Friesland) into the realm.

By all accounts, the Danes were very well aware of the slaughter that Charlemagne—in the name of the Church—had carried out on their pagan kinfolk, the Frisians and the Saxons. In any event, the Danish king Godfred, provoking Charlemagne into war, waged a seaborne assault on Friesland. The Viking raids on Charlemagne's empire—and on its wealthy churches and monasteries—can be seen as a heathen reprisal. It can also be seen as a classic power struggle between two empire builders. As Einhard wrote, "King Godfred was so puffed with vain aspirations that he counted on gaining empire over all Germany and looked upon Saxony and Frisia as his provinces."

In 810 A.D. Charlemagne—now Roman Emperor—began a march to meet Godfred, king of the Norsemen. It would be the emperor's final campaign. It was also an aborted one because Godfred was murdered by his own bodyguard before he could actually clash with Charlemagne.

REFORM
AND
RENAISSANCE

The two civilizations that had had the most lasting cultural influences on Western Europe, the Greek and Roman Empires, both virtually disintegrated by the time Charlemagne's ancestors came to power. Indeed, with the fall of the Roman Empire, Europeans had become largely illiterate. This decline in education spawned an era of intellectual indifference. Scholarly pursuits and social achievements quickly fell by the wayside.

Charlemagne's accomplishments are therefore all the more remarkable—and remarkably enlightened for the times. From the law to education to social improvements to public works, he was a tireless innovator and reformer. A noble man in all senses of the word, Charlemagne used his keen intellect and determination in the service of his people, whether rich or poor.

This period of cultural revival has been called the Carolingian Renaissance—kind of a precursor to the Renaissance of the 14th to

After the decline of the Greek and Roman Empires, Western civilization had reached a low point in terms of education and enlightenment. With the population of Europe mostly illiterate, Charlemagne spearheaded what would be known as the Carolingian Renaissance, which saw Charlemagne encouraging education and interest in the arts among his people.

17th centuries, which marked the true end of the medieval era. During this period, Charlemagne inspired a flowering of the arts, learning, and social transformation, which would continue with his successors—at least for a while.

Had he lived at a later time, Charlemagne may well have headed up a huge multinational corporation. He probably would have been enormously successful at it, too. What he seems to have most preferred more than fighting was administration. Apparently waging war was basically something that he felt he *had* to do to accomplish his goals. Will Durant, in *The Story of Civilization,* holds that Charlemagne

> had taken to the field to force some unity of government and faith upon a Western Europe torn for centuries past by conflicts of tribe and creed. He had now brought under his rule all the peoples between the Vistula and the Atlantic, between the Baltic and the Pyrenees, with nearly all of Italy and much of the Balkans. How could one man competently govern so vast and varied a realm? He was strong enough in body and nerves to bear a thousand responsibilities, perils, and crises. . . . He could [en]vision large purposes and could will the means as well as wish the ends. He could lead an army, persuade an assembly, humor the nobility, dominate the clergy, rule a harem.

Charlemagne ruled, of course, over many different conquered peoples in his realm. He dealt with these diverse cultures by utilizing two sets of laws: imperial decrees (called *capitularies,* Latin for "chapter") and local laws. Each group was allowed to live according to its own local laws, as they had been doing before becoming a part of the Frankish kingdom. Scholars were sent to interview the tribal chieftains and elders. They then wrote down the laws, which Charlemagne had published. Superceding the local laws were the royal decrees. These capitularies—numbering 65 in all—were wide ranging and addressed every aspect of life in Charlemagne's realm. They legislated everything from land ownership, military service, agriculture, and finance to morality, marriage and sexual life, and, of course, religion.

Charlemagne instituted many sweeping changes in his

government that overhauled the administrative system of his empire. For example, he enhanced the existing policy of *feudalism*—land given by the king to his noblemen to ensure their loyalty and service. In addition, he appointed certain nobles—either family members or loyal comrades—as provincial governors in charge of the various divisions of the kingdom. They were called *dukes* (an old Roman title from the Latin word for leader). Reporting to the dukes were the *counts,* who headed up individual districts called *counties.* These counts were essentially kings of their respective domains, having all of the administrative, judicial, and military authority of Charlemagne.

Each church also had its own district, or *diocese.* It was supervised by a bishop who, like the count, had authority over his district—in this case regarding all church-related matters. Counts and bishops, all vassals of the emperor, were in turn overseen by representatives of Charlemagne called *missi dominici* (Latin for "servants of the lord"). Their job was to supervise economic and legal matters in the emperor's name. These *missi,* as they were known, traveled all through the empire in pairs—one man from the Church, the other a layman. This theoretically ensured that the interests of one side wouldn't take precedence over the other. To further ensure impartiality, the missi were posted away from home so that their loyalties wouldn't be tested. Plus they were periodically moved to different places, to make even more certain that local ties wouldn't develop. After all, these missi had been chosen to serve their king, not the locals.

Every year both counts and bishops attended a general assembly at Charlemagne's court at Aachen (in modern Germany), where they would advise the emperor and hear his directives. Many directives were dealt with in Charlemagne's capitularies. *The Capitulary of Charlemagne Issued in the Year 802 A.D.,* for example, begins by laying out strict rules of behavior for the emperor's envoys, his missi.

One of the changes Charlemagne made was to enhance the existing policy of *seignorialism*, in which men were governed by regional leaders, and *feudalism*, in which land and labor were bestowed upon nobles in return for their service and loyalty. This illustration depicts a leader bestowing such authority to another in a feudal ceremony.

As given in the translation by the Avalon Project at Yale Law School, Charlemagne begins this capitulary by basically flattering these ambassadors:

Chapter I: Concerning the Embassy
Sent Out by the Lord Emperor.

The most serene and most Christian emperor Charles did choose from among his nobles the most prudent and the wisest men, archbishops as well as other bishops and venerable abbots and pious laymen, and did send them over his whole kingdom; and did grant through them, by means of all the following provisions, that men should live according to law and right. . . .

Charlemagne then lays down the law—and holds up strict standards:

> And let no one, through his cleverness or astuteness—as many are accustomed to do—dare to oppose the written law, or the sentence passed upon him, or the judicial sentence passed upon him, or to prevail against the churches of God or the poor or widows or minors or any Christian man. But all shall live together according to the precept of God in a just manner and under just judgment, and each one should be admonished to live in unity with the others in his occupation or calling. . . . And let the messengers diligently investigate all cases where any man claims that injustice has been done to him by any one . . . And thus, altogether and everywhere and in all cases, whether the matter concerns the holy churches of God or the poor or wards and widows or the whole people, let them fully administer law and justice according to the will and to the fear of God. . . . Nor should anyone be kept back from the right path of justice by the adulation or the reward of any man, by the obstacle of any relationship, or by the fear of powerful persons.

"Chapter II: Concerning the Fealty to be Promised to the Lord Emperor" deals with the loyalty of his subjects—which was demanded of "every man in his whole kingdom, ecclesiastic or layman . . . down to those under 12 years of age"— now that he had become emperor. In this chapter his counts are taken to task about military service (apparently even in medieval times people used influence and/or graft to escape the draft!):

> 7. That no one shall presume to neglect a summons to arms from the emperor; and that no count [should] be so presumptuous as to dare to release out of regard for any relationship, or on account of flattery or of any one's gift, any one of those who owe military service.

This same capitulary also argues for everyone getting a fair trial, with no shady behind-the-scenes manipulations, and being up on the fine points of the law:

> 9. That no man shall make a practice of unjustly carrying on the defense of another in court, whether from any cupidity [greed], being not a very great pleader; or in order, by the cleverness of his defense, to impede a just judgment, or, his case being a weak one, by a desire of oppressing. But each man, with regard to his own case or tax or debt, must carry on his own defense, unless he be infirm or ignorant of pleading—for which sort of persons the missi, or those who preside in that court, or a judge who knows the case for the defendant, shall plead before the court. . . . And this shall be done in every way according to the law so that justice shall be in no way impeded by any gift, payment, or by any wile of evil adulation or out of regard for any relationship. . . .

The 802 A.D. capitulary also decrees how the clergy should behave. It even spells out quite candidly the problems that have clearly beset the Church for millennia:

> 11. That bishops, abbots, and abbesses, who are placed in power over others, should strive to surpass in veneration and diligence those subject to them; that they should not oppress them with severe and tyrannous rule but should carefully guard the flock committed to them, with simple love, with mercy and charity, and by the example of good works. . . .

> 17. That the monks, moreover, shall live firmly and strictly according to the rule; since we know that whoever is lukewarm in carrying out His will is displeasing to God. As John, in the Apocalypse, bears witness: "I would that thou wert cold or hot. So then, because thou are lukewarm, I

will spue thee out of my mouth." They shall on no account take upon themselves secular occupations. They shall not be permitted to go outside of the monastery unless great necessity compels them; . . . Let them altogether avoid drunkenness and feasting; for it is known to all that chiefly through them one comes to be polluted by lust. For the very pernicious rumour has come to our ears that many, in the monasteries, have been taken in fornication in abomination and uncleanness. And most of all it saddens and disturbs us that it can be said without error that from those things whence the greatest hope of salvation for all Christians is believed to arise—namely, the manner of living and the chastity of the monks—the evil has arisen that some of the monks are found to be sodomites.

On the other hand, the gravity of some of the directives have been lost over time. By today's standards they're good for a chuckle—or a head scratch. For example:

19. That no bishops, abbots, priests, deacons—no one, in short, belonging to the clergy—shall presume to have hunting dogs or hawks, falcons, or sparrow-hawks. . . . Any one who presumes to do this . . . shall know that he loses his standing. Furthermore, he shall suffer such punishment for this, that others shall fear to wrongfully do likewise.

As regards such punishment, prior to Charlemagne, penalties for crimes were usually harsh and cruel. Trial by fire and trial by combat were the norm, as was mutilation and an eye-for-an-eye justice. By contrast, the goal of Charlemagne's jury system was restitution, not punishment. True, severe punishment was still carried out as a deterrent to other would-be criminals, but compensating those who had been robbed or cheated was ultimately the far better solution. After all, cutting off a thief's hand and giving it to

Before Charlemangne implemented the jury system of justice, judgments were usually carried out by trial by combat. In trial by combat, the victor would be declared vindicated by God and thus be found innocent, similar in some ways to Roman gladiator combat.

the person who had been wronged didn't really help the victim in any way.

Charlemagne even instituted the concept of a court of appeals. When complaints about unfairness or misconduct by either the missi or the *jurata* (a sworn jury of inquisitors) were brought to the king's attention, he assembled a court in each province to hear each case and deliver a new—or perhaps support the old—judgment. And so the trial-and-appeal system came into being.

But for all that he was an enlightened man of the time, Charlemagne still *was* a man of his time. And while he espoused equal justice for all, this did not necessarily include pagans or Jews.

In his *Capitulary for Saxony* (775–790), Charlemagne reserves the worst kind of punishment for anyone not toeing the Christian line. As translated by the *Medieval Sourcebook,* one directive commands:

> If any one, out of contempt for Christianity, shall have despised the holy Lenten fast and shall have eaten flesh, let him be punished by death.

Cremation of a body ("in accordance with pagan rites") was also an offense punishable by death. And:

> If any one of the race of Saxons hereafter concealed among them shall have wished to hide himself unbaptized and shall have scorned to come to baptism and shall have wished to remain a pagan, let him be punished by death.

In his *Capitulary for the Jews* (814), Charlemagne commands:

> Let no Jew presume to take in pledge or for any debt any of the goods of the Church in gold, silver, or other form, from any Christian. But if he presume to do so, which God forbid, let all his goods be seized and let his right hand be cut off.

The emperor then instructs:

> Concerning the oath of the Jews against the Christians: Place sorrel twice around his body from head to feet; he ought to stand when he takes his oath, and he should have in his right hand the five books of Moses according to his law, and if he cannot have them in Hebrew, he shall have them in Latin. "May the God who gave the law to Moses on Mount Sinai help me, and may the leprosy of Naamon the Syrian come upon me as it came upon him, and may the earth swallow me as it swallowed Dathan and Abiron, I have not committed evil against you in this cause."

Perhaps the most significant of all of Charlemagne's accomplishments—and arguably the most long lasting—

was the resurgence of education during his reign. And probably no other aspect of cultural life excited Charlemagne as education did. He was himself only semiliterate. But he had enormous admiration for scholarship and the arts, and he greatly encouraged learning among the citizens of his realm. He saw education as a means to both unify his people and create unity in the Frankish church. And his school at Aachen (Aix-la-Chapelle) became a beacon for scholars.

Charlemagne's dedication to scholarship began under his own palace roof. The king, his wife, and his children were among the first pupils. Charlemagne was determined that all of his children be well educated in the liberal arts — his daughters as well as his sons. This was extremely unusual at a time when virtually no women were schooled in anything but domestic skills. The king himself studied science, law, literature, theology, rhetoric, and astronomy, among other subjects.

He also invited other students from his kingdom to be educated at the school. Initially the school was limited to the sons of noblemen, but Charlemagne felt that every child of his realm should have the chance to learn, and he opened up the school to students of all classes. In fact, he felt that the poor children were better students than the rich ones. An anecdote relayed by a biographer known as the Monk of Saint Gall (usually identified as Notker Balbulus, who died in 912) deals with this notion in this translation from the *Medieval Sourcebook*:

> [W]hen Charles came back, after a long absence, crowned with victory, into Gaul, he ordered the [students] to come before him and present to him letters and verses of their own composition. Now, the boys of middle or low birth presented him with writings garnished with the sweet savours of wisdom beyond all that he could have hoped, while those of the children of noble parents were silly and

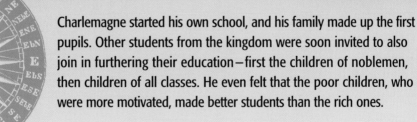

Charlemagne started his own school, and his family made up the first pupils. Other students from the kingdom were soon invited to also join in furthering their education—first the children of noblemen, then children of all classes. He even felt that the poor children, who were more motivated, made better students than the rich ones.

tasteless. Then the most wise Charles . . . addressed them in these words: "My children, you have found much favour with me because you have tried with all your strength to carry out my orders and win advantage for yourselves. . . and I will give you bishoprics and splendid monasteries, and you shall be always honourable in my eyes." Then he turned severely to [the privileged students] . . . and he flung at them in scorn these terrible words: "You nobles, you sons of my chiefs, you superfine dandies, you have trusted to your birth and your possessions and have set at naught my orders to your own advancement: You have neglected the pursuit of learning and you have given yourselves over to luxury and sport, to idleness and profitless pastimes." Then solemnly he raised his august head . . . and thus thundered against them, "By the King of Heaven, I take no account of your noble birth and your fine looks, though others may admire you for them. Know this for certain, that unless you make up for your former sloth by vigourous study, you will never get any favour from Charles."

To jump-start a revival of learning, Charlemagne arranged to have some of the most renowned scholars of the day come to teach at his court. The king had officially located his headquarters in the town of Aachen. Heretofore, Charlemagne didn't have a permanent residence. In the winter he would hold court in one palace or another, then go elsewhere for the summer. But in 794 the king decided to permanently locate his court in Aachen—in large measure because of the warm springs there. (The court church, which Charlemagne had built partly from materials imported from Rome and Ravenna, still stands today.) Aachen soon became an important educational center as well.

The scholars who gathered at Aachen were primarily devoted to art, literature, and philosophy. Charlemagne honored them with key positions of responsibility. Historians have noted that one valuable task of these scholars—most of whom were monks because they were usually the only members of society who knew how to write—was to keep learning alive by recopying classical literature and other ancient texts. In fact, many of the scholars who gathered at the palace to further their own education did so specifically to use the enormous library that was being amassed.

(That these works have survived to modern times is directly due to Charlemagne's devotion to preserving them. According to historian Dr. E. L. Knox, "Almost 90 percent of the works of ancient Rome that we possess exist in their earliest form in a Carolingian manuscript, and almost nothing that survived up to [the year] 800 has subsequently been lost." Such an incredible achievement is entirely due to Charlemagne's love of learning.)

Charlemagne was lucky enough to be in northern Italy at the same time as a Benedictine monk named Albin Alcuin (c. 732–804). This Anglo-Saxon scholar came from the English town of York. The library there had a huge collection of classical manuscripts. Charlemagne persuaded the monk to come to Aachen, where he became, in essence, the minister of education. Alcuin's main task was to design a course of study for the palace school. The intent of the monk's curriculum was to train students—priests and monks, especially—to develop what today would be called their critical-thinking skills.

Alcuin modeled his educational program on the classical Roman system. However, being Anglo-Saxon himself, Alcuin's curriculum also incorporated cultural elements from the Irish and—ironically, given Charlemagne's thorny history with them—the Saxons. This cross-cultural exchange of ideas was significant because during the eighth century, Ireland and Britain were culturally leaps and bounds ahead of France. Alcuin's course of study has come down to us as the seven liberal arts, which are still studied in colleges today. These are divided into the *trivium*, made up of grammar (how to write), rhetoric (how to speak), and logic (how to think), and the *quadrivium,* which comprises geometry, arithmetic, astronomy, and music. The classical education that Alcuin established required students to read the literary and philosophical works of Homer, Virgil, Horace, Plato, and Cicero, among others.

Aside from Alcuin, scholars at the court included Peter from Pisa, a noted grammarian; Paul the Deacon, a historian from Italy; Teodulf, a Visigoth from Spain, who not only developed teaching at all levels and established libraries, but also improved the realm's justice system; and, of course, Einhard, the royal biographer, who was a homegrown Frank. These men are just a few of the intellectuals who came from all parts of the empire to teach at Charlemagne's schools. From these schools would come the great universities of Europe.

One of Charlemagne's capitularies dated 787 A.D. pushed monks to establish schools in cathedrals and monasteries where both the clergy and the laity could study. Two years later yet another capitulary advised the schools' directors to "take care to make no difference between the sons of serfs and of freeman, so that they might come and sit on the same benches to study grammar, music, and arithmetic." Yet another capitulary of 805 provided for medical education. Charlemagne's directives were apparently most successful. According to Will Durant in *The Story of Civilization*:

> That his appeals were not fruitless appears from the many cathedral or monastic schools that now sprang up in France and western Germany. Theodulf, Bishop of Orleans, organized schools in every parish of his diocese, welcomed all children to them, and forbade the priest instructors to take any fees; this is the first instance in history of free and general education.

Charlemagne's promotion of learning was due in part to his devotion to Christianity. He felt that being educated "opened a person to the religious knowledge that made for salvation of the soul," and Charlemagne hoped to raise the level of religious observance and morality in his kingdom. Clergymen and monks were also a focus of Charlemagne's educational efforts. He saw to it that monastic schools were set up throughout his empire. This enabled the intensive study of Latin and literature, for above all, Charlemagne wanted unity in the Frankish Church.

Many of the clergy were barely literate, and even the monks, many of whom spent their whole lives transcribing ancient manuscripts, could barely read. They often merely copied the texts by rote and couldn't read or understand what they were transcribing. Errors had occurred from copying poor handwriting or previously written mistakes, and this confusion was passed on. (It has been said that Charlemagne wasn't able to find a single good copy of the Bible anywhere in his kingdom.) The king decided that basically the monks needed to start from scratch. All the mistakes in the manuscripts first had to be corrected before any more copies were made. Charlemagne had Alcuin develop a new standard style of writing. It came to be termed "Caroligian miniscule," or "Carolingian script." This handwriting style introduced elements that we take for granted: punctuation, upper- and lower-case letters, and even separation between words. Previous texts were all upper case, without punctuation, and the words often ran together. Add to this the poor lighting and primitive writing instruments that the monks had to endure, and it's a wonder *anything* got written down correctly! (One of Charlemagne's ordinances directed toward the transcribing monks is called *On Scribes: That They Should Not Write Corruptly.*) The new script, which uses clear, neat letters and words distinct from one another, is the one we still use today—the one you are reading at this moment. And not only were the Bible and other sacred works of the Church copied by the monks, but also copied classical writings.

Monks used to copy manuscripts without even being able to read what they were transcribing. Thus even errors were copied down without being fixed. Charlemagne decided that there needed to be a standard style of writing, which included employing spaces between distinct words (instead of having them all run together, as they would in previous texts).

Charlemagne also saw to it that Latin was standardized. In a letter to Abbot Baugaulf of Fulda (known as *De litteris colendis*, or "the study of letters"), which dates from around 785, he called for reforms in the Latin language. It was the king's belief that for a thought to be right, the wording—its form and language—had to be appropriate. The thousand-year-old language had seen new words and phrases introduced over time that needed to be incorporated uniformly. Latin was, of course, the Romans' native language. As they conquered various countries, they spread their language throughout their empire.

After the collapse of Rome, the mother tongue turned into dozens of provincial dialects. These dialects had evolved over time when Latin was absorbed by the conquered peoples. The dialects further evolved when barbarians later overran the empire. These tribes weren't usually successful in imposing their own languages on the (by then) Romanized locals. But they did cause many variations in the local idioms. As a result, by Charlemagne's day the changes in Latin had become so great that in much of Europe, the common people could no longer understand church sermons. As a result, Charlemagne decreed that from that point on sermons were to given in the *lingua latina rustica* (the "country-folk's Latin"). That is to say, the sermons had to be spoken in the local language. During this time the first writings that were truly identifiable as French, then Spanish, and then Italian—our modern Romance (literally, "the Roman's") languages—were composed.

During his years on the throne, Charlemagne ruled over the most enlightened, just government that Western Europe had ever known. He legislated for everything from finance and industry to agriculture to morals. But perhaps the most important changes that Charlemagne sought to bring about were for the peasantry. From his many innovations evolved some of our most fundamental ideas of governmental rule.

Charlemagne held semiannual assemblies of property owners. There he would submit his proposals for changes in legislation, which would be voted on by the assembly. At these meetings, too, inquiries were sometimes made of the foremost citizens, whose replies were given under oath, about the state of their district—its "taxable wealth, the state of public order, the existence of crimes or criminals." The verdict of the jurata decided land ownership disputes or criminal guilt.

These inquirers were chosen from common citizens, not the nobility. The jurata was the basis for what has become our standard jury system: a jury of one's peers.

Furthermore, some four centuries before England created its Magna Carta—the groundbreaking charter of 1215 that guaranteed certain rights and privileges for British nobles—Charlemagne established the *Capitulare missorum*, which guaranteed rights and privileges to *all* the people of his realm.

Though the term didn't actually exist for another thousand years, feudalism was basically developed during Charlemagne's reign. To organize his far-flung empire, Charlemagne had created the relatively self-ruling provinces overseen by his royal representatives, the dukes and counts. The lands therein were to be farmed by a free class of peasants, or serfs, who would pay rent to the nobles. In theory—and it was Charlemagne's intention—this arrangement would provide the peasants with a degree of self-sufficiency. It didn't work out that way. The serfs often became virtual servants to their overlords. To rectify this situation, Charlemagne established a welfare system. Taxes were levied on the nobility, and those monies were put into a relief fund for the poor.

The expression "the coin of the realm" is often used as a figure of speech. But prior to Charlemagne's reign, it wouldn't have signified much because the use of coins had all but disappeared with the fall of the Roman Empire. Charlemagne decided to revive the widespread use of coinage. Gold was becoming increasingly rare, so he minted silver coins, the silver Denars, in place of gold coins. (All the coins bore his likeness—just as the old Roman coins had been stamped with Caesar's face.) His money would serve as samples for all western coinage for the next 500 years. Moreover, his monetary system would stay valid in Great Britain until 1971: 1 pound = 20 shillings = 240 pennies.

Aside from bringing back coins as a method of payment, Charlemagne reorganized his empire's economy. Customs fees and tolls were standardized. Weights and measures were also made consistent, which made trade easier. In fact, Charlemagne encouraged foreign trade and enjoyed friendly relations with the kings of England and Scotland and the caliph of Baghdad—despite the fact that Persia was a Muslim country. (This seeming contradiction was typical of Charlemagne. Although he was devoutly, even ferociously, Christian and would fight to the death to defend his borders against "the infidels," he saw nothing wrong in being their trading partner—or giving them and receiving from them generous gifts—and even going to their defense if the occasion called for it.) In *The Life of Charlemagne,* Einhard relates:

> His relations with Aaron [Harun al-Rashid], King of the Persians, who ruled over almost the whole of the East, India excepted, were so friendly that this prince preferred his favor to that of all the kings and potentates of the earth, and considered that to him alone marks of honor and munificence were due. Accordingly, when the ambassadors sent by Charles to visit the most holy sepulcher and place of resurrection of our Lord and Savior presented themselves before [al-Rashid] with gifts, and made known their master's wishes, he not only granted what was asked, but gave possession of that holy and blessed spot. When they returned, he dispatched his ambassadors with them, and sent magnificent gifts . . . of the Eastern lands. A few years before this Charles had asked him for an elephant, and he sent the only one that he had. . . .

Charlemagne further boosted the economy of his realm by encouraging his citizens to use better farming methods so that they might have better yields from their crops.

The king—later, the emperor—also seems to have been an inveterate builder. According to Einhard:

> [Charlemagne] . . . undertook also very many works calculated to adorn and benefit his kingdom, and brought several of them to completion. Among these, the most deserving of mention are the basilica of the Holy Mother of God at Aix-la-Chapelle, built in the most admirable manner, and a bridge over the Rhine at Mayence, half a mile long, the breadth of the river at this point. This bridge was destroyed by fire [May 813] the year before Charles died, but, owing to his death so soon after, could not be repaired, although he had intended to rebuild it in stone. He began two palaces of beautiful workmanship— one near his manor . . . not far from Mayence; the other at Nimeguen. . . . But above all, sacred edifices were the object of his care throughout his whole kingdom; and whenever he found them falling to ruin from age, he commanded the priests and fathers who had charge of them to repair them, and made sure by commissioners that his instructions were obeyed.

Charlemagne's most ambitious public-works project, which was never built, called for the creation of a canal that would connect the Rhine and Danube Rivers. (A Rhine-Danube canal, which runs 421 miles, or 677 kilometers, was eventually constructed—though not until 1992. It cost 6 billion German Deutschmarks to build and transports goods more cheaply than by road—just as Charlemagne knew it would.)

The arts—in all of its forms—were also important to Charlemagne. He had valuable works of art from Italy brought back to his kingdom so that people would once again appreciate sculptures and paintings. But he especially loved music. For example, to ensure that old folk songs that celebrated the deeds of ancient kings would not be lost, he had them transcribed for posterity.

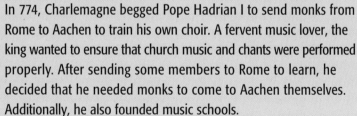

In 774, Charlemagne begged Pope Hadrian I to send monks from Rome to Aachen to train his own choir. A fervent music lover, the king wanted to ensure that church music and chants were performed properly. After sending some members to Rome to learn, he decided that he needed monks to come to Aachen themselves. Additionally, he also founded music schools.

Church music in particular, though, stirred him. Charlemagne was determined that chants and other church music would be performed according to proper tradition. Accordingly, he had several choir members go to Rome to learn at the source. But deciding that this wasn't sufficient, he begged Pope Hadrian I in 774 to send two monks to the court at Aachen to train his homegrown choir members. The pope consented, and these monks brought about a return to the original form of the Gregorian chant—and also preserved the manuscripts on which they were written. In 789 Charlemagne addressed a decree to the whole clergy of his empire, instructing every member to properly learn and perform the *Cantus Romanus* [Roman chant]. Charlemagne's agents and representatives were ordered to watch over the faithful, carrying out his orders regarding music.

Charlemagne also founded schools of music in France and throughout Germany. Trained singers from famous choirs in Rome were placed in charge of these institutions. They apparently were rather shocked at first by the barbarism of their pupils. One noted that his students' notion of singing in church was to howl like wild beasts. Another, Johannes Didimus, in his *Life of Gregory,* declared: "These gigantic bodies, whose voices roar like thunder, cannot imitate our sweet tones, for their barbarous and ever-thirsty throats can only produce sounds as harsh as those of a loaded wagon passing over a rough road."

Another example of Charlemagne's love of music—and his generosity—can be found in a story told by Notker Balbulus, the Monk of Saint Gall, as translated by the *Medieval Sourcebook:*

> When Charles one day came in his journeyings to a certain palace, a certain clerk from among the wandering monks entered the choir, and being completely ignorant of these rules was soon forced to remain stupid and silent among the singers. Thereupon the choirmaster raised his wand and threatened to strike him unless he went on singing. Then the poor clerk, not knowing what to do or where to turn, and not daring to go out, twisted his neck into the shape of a bow and with open mouth and distended cheeks did his utmost to imitate the appearance of a singer. All the rest could not

restrain their laughter, but the most valiant emperor, whose mind was never shaken from its firm base even by great events, seemed not to notice his mockery of singing and, pitying his struggles and his anxiety, soothed his fears with these words: "Many thanks, good clerk, for your singing and your efforts." Then he ordered a pound of silver to be given him to relieve his poverty.

THE
LEGACY OF
CHARLEMAGNE

When Charlemagne was anointed as emperor in St. Peter's Basilica in Rome on Christmas Day 799, it actually did very little in terms of increasing his real power. It wasn't a turning point in either his personal life or the life of his realm. In fact, although he was now officially the Emperor of the Roman Empire, he never again returned to Rome itself.

But the title was an important political move. Charlemagne was now officially the head of the greatest empire in the Western world. Being "the most sere Augustus, crowned by God, great, pacific emperor, governing the Roman Empire, and, through the mercy of God, king of the Franks and Lombards" (as a decree signed May 29, 801, declared) suddenly put Charlemagne on a par with Emperor Michael I of Byzantium. This equality served the new emperor well in 805. Though the Byzantine emperor wasn't happy when Charlemagne was crowned, Michael was forced to recognize Charlemagne's

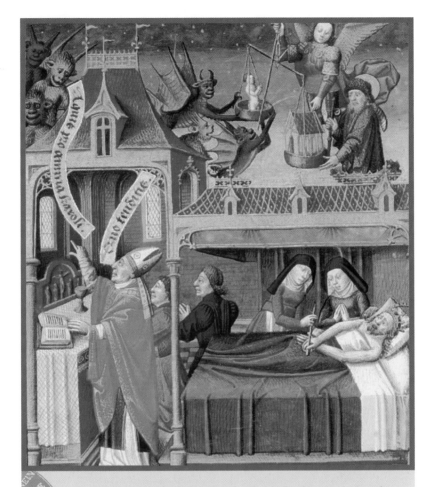

An illustration depicting the death of Charlemagne. People at the time put great faith in superstition and cosmic events such as lunar and solar eclipses, sunspots, natural disasters, and so on. Charlemagne dismissed these events as pointing toward his own demise, although he was all too aware of their significance.

title in exchange for the territories of Venetia (Venice), Istria, and Dalmatia (both part of modern-day Croatia). This peaceful exchange avoided war and improved relations between the two powers.

But the days of acquiring new territories had essentially

passed by the time of the emperor's elevation. Given the geography of his empire, expansion really couldn't advance much beyond the borders that had been reached by 800. There were also fewer enemies to conquer. The Normans, though, were making periodic raids by sea on Frank coastal villages. To combat this threat, Charlemagne called for a new navy to be built. And in 810, a campaign was begun against the Normans— with Charlemagne taking the elephant that his friend the Caliph of Baghdad had given him. That conflict finally ended—but only because the Norman king died, not because of Charlemagne's superior battle skills. Still, many of the skirmishes that took place in the period between Charlemagne's coronation and his death were fought by his sons. In 801, Louis (also known as Louis the Pious) captured Barcelona. And in 806, his son Carloman (also known as Charles the Younger) defeated the Wends, a Slavish tribe whose homeland was in modern-day East Germany.

But not only had Charlemagne's greatest triumphs and achievements already been realized, the empire was already starting to flounder. According to historian Joel F. Harrington:

> Despite its claim as the successor to the Western Roman Empire, Charlemagne's realm lacked many of the important institutions that had allowed the old Roman Empire to survive the emperor's death. Institutions such as a money economy, a strong governmental infrastructure [that could oversee such things as maintaining the roads and a system of communication], and a professional civil service were needed to keep the empire from disintegrating. [It also lacked a standing army and a navy for coastal defense to defend the kingdom against foreign invaders.] Instead, the empire was based almost entirely on Charlemagne's own ability to hold together a large number of different tribes and ethnic groups. The size of the empire made it difficult to administer, and tribal dissension was a frequent threat.

Charlemagne's sons Carloman, Pepin (not shown) and Louis were to take over his realm. Unfortunately, Pepin died in 810, and Carloman died in 811, leaving Louis to be the sole ruler. In 813, Charlemagne proclaimed Louis to be king and emperor, and the two ruled jointly until Charlemagne's death in 814.

Though the Frankish law of inheritance had been nothing but problematic for his ancestors, Charlemagne nonetheless planned to split his kingdom among his three remaining sons rather than try to retain its unity. He therefore prepared a will in 806 A.D. that would have divided the realm as follows: The oldest, Carloman (or Charles), would receive Frankland proper—Saxony, Frisia, Franconia, and Hesse; Pepin would be given Lombardy, Bavaria, and Southern Alemanni; and Louis's share would be most of what today is France. But as fate would have it, Pepin died in 810, and then Carloman died in 811, leaving Louis to inherit the whole empire when his father died. (Unfortunately for the empire, Louis—called Louis the Pious—was more suited for a spiritual life than a worldly one. To most observers he seemed quite unsuited, even unfit, to govern the world his father was leaving him.)

It appears that Charlemagne's final years were filled with troubles—beginning with the elephant that he took on his Norman campaign, which died during the fight. As noted, his son Pepin died in 810; his daughter Hrodrud died that year as well. And that same year the empire suffered a cattle plague, resulting in widespread famine. These cruel blows seem to have affected the emperor's health, which began to decline. Then, making matters even worse, Carloman died the following year.

By 813, Charlemagne was a man broken in spirit and health. Apparently sensing that his end was nearing, he summoned Louis, his only remaining son, to the court. He also gathered together the most important officials in the empire. In September of that year, Charlemagne placed the crown on his son's head and proclaimed Louis the Pious as King of the Franks and Emperor of the Romans. The two would rule jointly until Charlemagne's death.

The ninth century was still a time of great superstition. Omens and portents were read into ordinary occurrences. According to Einhard, writing in *The Life of Charlemagne*:

> Very many omens had portended [Charlemagne's] approaching end, a fact that he had recognized as well as others. Eclipses both of the sun and moon were very frequent during the last three years of his life, and a black spot was visible

on the sun for the space of seven days. The gallery between the basilica and the palace, which he had built at great pains and labor, fell in sudden ruin to the ground on the day of the Ascension of our Lord. The wooden bridge over the Rhine at Mayence, which he had caused to be constructed with admirable skill, at the cost of ten years' hard work, so that it seemed as if it might last forever, was so completely consumed in three hours by an accidental fire that not a single splinter of it was left, except what was under water. Moreover, one day in his last campaign into Saxony against Godfred, King of the Danes, [Charlemagne] himself saw a ball of fire fall suddenly from the heavens with a great light. . . . It rushed across the clear sky from right to left, and . . . the horse which he was riding gave a sudden plunge . . . and threw him to the ground so heavily that . . . his sword belt shattered. . . . Again, the palace at Aix-la-Chapelle frequently trembled, . . . the basilica in which he was afterwards buried was struck by lightning, and the gilded ball that adorned the pinnacle of the roof was shattered by the thunderbolt and hurled upon the bishop's house adjoining. . . . But [Charlemagne] despised, or affected to despise, all these omens as having no reference whatever to him.

After the coronation, Charlemagne sent his son back to Aquitania. Although weak, the aging emperor decided to spend time pursuing one of his favorite pastimes: hunting. He spent the rest of the autumn "in the chase" and finally returned to the palace around the beginning of November 813. The following January he was afflicted with a high fever and took to his bed on January 22. Einhard records Charlemagne's last days and his final journey:

As soon as he was taken sick, he prescribed for himself abstinence from food, as he always used to do in case of fever, thinking that the disease could be driven off, or at least mitigated, by fasting. Besides the fever, he suffered from a pain the side, which the Greeks call pleurisy; but he still persisted in fasting and in keeping up his strength only by [drinks] taken at very long intervals. He died January twenty-eighth, the seventh day from the time that he took to his bed, at nine o'clock in the morning, after partaking of the holy communion, in the seventy-second year of his age and the forty-seventh of his reign.

His body was washed and cared for in the usual manner, and was then carried to the church and interred amid the greatest lamentations of all the people. There was some question at first where to lay him because in his lifetime he had given no directions as to his burial; but at length all agreed that he could nowhere be more honorably entombed than in the very basilica that he had built in the town at his own expense, for love of God and our Lord Jesus Christ, and in honor of the Holy and Eternal Virgin, His Mother. He was buried there the same day that he died [in his imperial robes], and a gilded arch was erected above his tomb with his image and an inscription. . . . "In this tomb lies the body of Charles, the Great and Orthodox Emperor, who gloriously extended the kingdom of the Franks, and reigned prosperously for forty-seven years. He died at the age of seventy [sic], in the year of our Lord 814, the 7th Indiction, on the 28th day of January."

Charlemagne's remarkable rule spanned 45 years—this at a time when an average *lifespan* was not even that long. Like so many rulers before him, he expected his kingdom to continue after his death. Sadly, his son Louis was a mere shadow of his father, and the empire Charlemagne had literally fought to put together soon began coming apart.

Louis died in 840. Before he did so, like his father, he made plans for the kingdom to once again be divided—this time between his own three sons.

Louis's sons were initially unhappy with the arrangement and waged war on each other after their father's death. They finally reached an amicable agreement in 843. This agreement is laid out in the Treaty of Verdun, which divides the realm into three equal, independent kingdoms. This treaty signified the beginning of dissolution of Charlemagne's empire into territories that foreshadowed the nations of modern-day Western Europe. Louis I received the East Frankish Kingdom (later Germany), Charles II (Charles the Bald) ruled over the West Frankish Kingdom (later France), and Lothar I received the Middle Frankish Kingdom (Belgium and the Netherlands, Luxembourg, Alsace, Lorraine, Burgundy, Switzerland, and most of Italy). Lothar also kept the basically meaningless title of Emperor. It wasn't until Charles's son Charles III (Charles the Fat) received the crown in 885 that the various kingdoms were reunited—for the final time.

Meanwhile, attacks on coastal villages by the Norse had gone from sporadic raids to all-out invasions. Soon whole regions, such as Frisia and Normandy, had slipped away from the empire. In the hundred years between 850 and 950 A.D., Vikings burned coastal towns, Muslim raids on Italy disrupted trade, and the Magyars attacked from the east. Charlemagne's beloved monasteries were plundered and burned. All of these invasions steadily chipped away at the realm. The once-mighty empire crumbled and splintered.

The Carolingian dynasty ruled until 888. Then Eudes (or Odo), son of Robert the Strong, wrested away the crown and was named King of West Francia. The Carolingians regained the crown when Charles the Simple was named king in 893. By handing over Normandy to the Vikings, he was able to retain the throne until 922, when he, too, was deposed. However, by then he had lost control of Burgundy and Aquitaine, as well. In 936 the Carolingians once again took the throne and ruled without interruption until 987.

Although Charlemagne's empire had already started to recede at the time of his death, his legacy is unparalleled to this day. His unification of the different tribes and cultures in Europe as well as his dedication to education and preservation of manuscripts all ushered in the dawn of European civilization.

They were then toppled for good by a stronger, more politically connected family—the Capetian dynasty—just as their own family had overthrown the Merovingians some two centuries before.

Although Charlemagne's empire barely outlived him, his legacy has continued to this day.

One of the poets at Charlemagne's court called him the Father of Europe. It is as good an appraisal as any. By combining Roman, German, Saxon, and Christian cultures, he fostered the beginning of European civilization. Furthermore, the greatest European unifiers—from Frederick Barbarossa to Napoleon and modern-day leaders such as Helmut Kohl and Gerhard Schröder—have all cited Charlemagne as spearheading European unification.

Certainly one of Charlemagne's greatest legacies is having established a tradition of learning. By offering free education to anyone in his realm, the emperor revolutionized the concept of learning. And because of his interest in preserving and reviving knowledge, hundreds, perhaps thousands, of ancient manuscripts were copied, saving them for posterity. European monasteries were firmly established as keepers of knowledge due in large measure to the determination of Emperor Charlemagne.

During his lifetime he would be universally known as Carolus Magnus or Karl der Grosse or Charlemagne: Charles the Great. It is truly a fitting epithet.

742 A.D. Pepin the Short's son Carolus, or Charles, is born April 2. The place of birth is not known for certain but is probably Aachen (Aix-la-Chapelle) in modern-day Garmany.

751 Pepin the Short dethrones the last Merovingian king and takes the throne for himself.

754 Pope Stephen crowns Pepin the Short as King of the Franks.

760+ Charlemagne accompanies his father during his military efforts to conquer the lands south the Loire River.

768 Pepin the Short dies, and his kingdom is divided up between his two sons, Charles and his younger brother, Carloman.

768± Charlemagne marries his first wife, Himiltrude. They have a son, Pepin (Pepin the Hunchback).

770 Charlemagne marries Desideria, daughter of the Lombard King Desiderius, at his mother's urging.

771 Carloman dies, and Charlemagne becomes sole King of the Franks.

771 Charlemagne divorces Desideria and marries Hildegarde of Swabia. They have seven children together, including Charles, King of France; Pepin, King of Italy; and Louis, King of France.

772 Charlemagne begins what would ultimately be a 33-year war against the Saxons.

774 Responding to the pope's request for help, Charlemagne invades and conquers Lombardy.

775 Charlemagne begins new attacks against the Saxons and their leader, Widukind.

778 Charlemagne invades Spain. He encounters the greatest defeat of his life, and the events later inspire the great French epic poem, *The Song of Roland.*

782 The Saxons launch an attack.

783 In response to the Saxon attack, Charlemagne orders the execution of 4,500 Saxon prisoners in one day. On April 30, Hildegarde dies in childbirth. Charlemagne's mother, Berthrada, dies three months later.

783   Charlemagne begins the final three-year campaign to conquer Saxony. He fights two pitched battles and routs the enemy so badly that they never again take the offensive against the king.

783   Charlemagne marries Fastrada, by whom he has two daughters.

788   Charlemagne conquers the Bavarians.

791–796   Charlemagne conquers the empire of the Avars (modern Hungary and Austria).

792   Pepin, Charlemagne's oldest son, conspires to dethrone his father. When his deceit is discovered, he is banished to a monastery.

794   Charlemagne marries his final, and favorite, wife, Luitgard.

795   On Christmas day, Pope Hadrian I dies, and Leo III is chosen as the new pope.

800   Leo III is brutally attacked during a religious procession in Rome. After returning to health, he implores Charlemagne to help him fight accusations against him. Charlemagne is successful in helping Leo regain his papal office.

800   In Saint Peter's Basilica in Rome, on Christmas Day, Pope Leo crowns Charlemagne Roman Emperor—the first person to have this title since the last emperor was deposed in 476 A.D.

802   Charlemagne settles his court at Aachen and gathers the best scholars in Western Europe to establish a school at the palace.

810   Pepin, Charlemagne's second son by Hildegarde, dies.

811   Charles the Younger, Charlemagne's oldest son by Hildegarde, dies.

813   Charlemagne crowns his only surviving son, Louis, emperor.

814   Charlemagne dies on January 28.

Arkenberg, Jerome S. "Arabs, Franks, and the Battle of Tours, 732: Three Accounts." *Internet Medieval Source Book,* 1998. *http://www.fordham.edu/halsall/source732.tours.html.*

Arkenberg, Jerome S. "Charlemagne: Capitulary for the Jews, 814." *Internet Medieval Source Book,* 1997. *http://www.fordham.edu/halsall/source/814capitul-jews.html.*

Bullfinch, Thomas. *Bullfinch's Mythology: The Age of Chivalry and Legends of Charlemagne or Romance of the Middle Ages.* New York: New American Library, 1962.

Classen, Peter. "Charlemagne 742–814." *Encyclopedia Britannica 2002.* *http://www.hfac.uh.edu/gbrown/philosophers/leibniz/BritannicaPages/Charlemagne/Charlemagne.html.*

Durant, Will. *The Story of Civilization, Part III: The Age of Faith.* New York: Simon & Schuster, 1935.

Einhard. *The Life of Charlemagne. Internet Medieval Source Book,* 1999. Translated by Samuel Epes Turner (New York: Harper & Brothers, 1880). *www.fordham.edu/halsall/basic/einhard.html.*

Gregory of Tours. *The History of the Franks: Books I–X. Internet Medieval Source Book,* 1997. *http://www.fordham.edu/halsall/basis/gregory-hist.html.*

Harrington, Joel F. "Charlemagne." *Microsoft Encarta Online Encyclopedia* 2002. *http://encarta.msn.com.*

Kampers, Franz. "Pepin the Short." *The Catholic Encyclopedia,* 1999. *http://www.newadvent.org.*

Kreis, Steven. "Charlemagne and the Carolingian Renaissance." *The History Guide,* 2000. *http://historyguide.org.*

Kurth, Godefroi. "The Franks." *The Catholic Encyclopedia,* 1999. *http://www.newadvent.org.*

Kurth, Godefroi. "Charles Martel." *The Catholic Encyclopedia,* 1999. *http://www.newadvent.org.*

Lasko, Peter. *The Kingdom of the Franks.* New York: McGraw-Hill, 1971.

Knox, Ellis L. "Charlemagne." *History of Western Civilization.* Boise State University. *http://history.boisestate.edu/westciv/charles/.*

Munro, D. C. Charlemagne: "Capitulary for Saxony 775–790."
   Internet Medieval Source Book, 1997.
   http://www.fordham.edu/halsall/carol-saxony.html.

Shahan, Thomas J., E. MacPherson. "Charlemagne."
   The Catholic Encyclopedia, 1999.
   http://www.newadvent.org.

Thorpe, Lewis. *The Two Lives of Charlemagne.* London: Penguin Books, 1969.

Bullfinch, Thomas. *Bullfinch's Mythology: The Age of Chivalry and Legends of Charlemagne or Romance of the Middle Ages.* New York: New American Library, 1962.

Bullough, Donald A. *The Age of Charlemagne.* New York: Putnam, 1966.

Collins, Roger. *Charlemagne.* Toronto: University of Toronto Press, 1998.

Durant, Will. *The Story of Civilization, Part III: The Age of Faith.* New York: Simon & Schuster, 1935.

Lasko, Peter. *The Kingdom of the Franks.* New York: McGraw-Hill, 1971.

Munz, Peter. *Life in the Age of Charlemagne.* New York: Capricorn Books, 1971.

Thorpe, Lewis. *The Two Lives of Charlemagne.* London: Penguin Books, 1969.

◆ WEB SITES ◆

Charlemagne the King: A biography from Will Durant's
   STORY OF CIVILIZATION, 1950
   http://www.chronique.com/Library/MedHistory/charlemagne.htm

Einhard. *The Life of Charlemagne. Internet Medieval Source Book,* 1999
   http://www.fordham.edu/halsall/basic/einhard.html

Gregory of Tours. *The History of the Franks: Books I–X.*
   Internet Medieval Source Book, 1997
   http://www.fordham.edu/halsall/basis/gregory-hist.html

page:

13:	Scala/Art Resource, NY	57:	Gianni Dagli Orti/Corbis
17:	Bettmann/Corbis	59:	Hierophant Collection
22:	Archivo Iconografico, S.A./Corbis	63:	Bettmann/Corbis
25:	Hierophant Collection	66:	Hierophant Collection
30:	Michael Nicholson/Corbis	70:	Hulton Archive/Getty Images
33:	Bettmann/Corbis	73:	Bettmann/Corbis
40:	Hierophant Collection	78:	Archivo Iconographico, S.A./Corbis
43:	Gianni Dagli Orti/Corbis	83:	Hulton-Deutsch Collection/Corbis
46:	Bettmann/Corbis	87:	Giraudon/Art Resource, NY
50:	Hulton Archive/Getty Images	89:	Stefano Bianchetti/Corbis
53:	Hulton Archive/Getty Images	94:	Archivo Iconographico, S.A./Corbis

Cover: Bettmann/Corbis
Frontis: Hierophant Collection

DALE EVVA GELFAND has worked in publishing for over 20 years as a freelance writer and editor. She is the author of a number of books about nature and gardening—including *Grow a Hummingbird Garden* and *Creating Habitat for Backyard Birds*—as well as a contributing writer for books on women's health and child raising. A self-professed history enthusiast, her interests lie primarily in the ancient, medieval, and Renaissance periods. This is both her first book on history and her first book for Chelsea House.

ARTHUR M. SCHLESINGER, JR. is the leading American historian of our time. He won the Pulitzer Prize for his book *The Age of Jackson* (1945) and again for a chronicle of the Kennedy Administration, *A Thousand Days* (1965), which also won the National Book Award. Professor Schlesinger is the Albert Schweitzer Professor of the Humanities at the City University of New York and has been involved in several other Chelsea House projects, including the series REVOLUTIONARY WAR LEADERS, COLONIAL LEADERS, and YOUR GOVERNMENT.